100
THINGS TO
KNOW ABOUT
SCIENCE

Written by
Alex Frith, Minna Lacey,
Jerome Martin & Jonathan Melmoth

Illustrated by
Federico Mariani
& Jorge Martin

What is science?

Science is a way of studying the world to find out how it works. Different scientists specialize in different areas to look for answers to all sorts of big questions...

What am I made of?

Nuclear physics

Microbiology

Food science

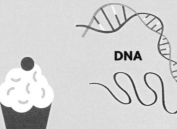

DNA

Paleontology

Chemistry

Evolutionary biology

How can I lift this more easily?

Where did people come from?

Mechanical engineering

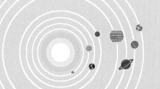
You can find definitions of scientific terms in the **glossary** on pages 115-119.

Cosmology

How did the universe begin?

What's the point of recycling?

Earth science

Petrochemicals

What's the fastest thing in the universe?

Solar science

Aerodynamics

What's it like under the oceans?

Often, science simply confirms things most people already knew. But, every day, scientists ask new questions – and they uncover surprising new facts all the time...

Oceanography

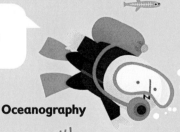

The universe is...

everything there is.

Sun

Earth
(not to scale)

Instruments on Earth can detect
just a tiny fraction of everything
in outer space, known as the
observable universe.

The edge of the entire universe –
if it has an edge at all – lies some
vast, unknown distance
away from Earth.

No one knows what shape the universe makes.

The universe is mind-bogglingly **vast**.
**And it's getting bigger
and bigger**
all the time.

2 Light years...
measure distance – not time.

The distance covered by a beam of light that travels for a year is known as **1 light year**.

After the Sun, Earth's next nearest star, Proxima Centauri, is around **4 light years** away.

Earth

Sun

Proxima Centauri

8 light minutes

1 light year

The edge of the observable universe is around **46 billion** light years away from Earth.

3 All life on Earth...

can be traced back to the same starting point.

Scientists classify living things into groups called **kingdoms**, shown here in capitals. These all evolved from one original kingdom, a group of organisms known as **prokaryotes**.

PLANTS
First appeared
about **480 million** years ago.

Number of known
species: **300,000**

ANIMALS
First appeared
about **580 million** years ago.

Invertebrates
(animals without backbones)
The oldest types of animals.
Number of known
species: **1.2 million**

Vertebrates
(animals with backbones)
First appeared around
525 million years ago.
Number of known
species: **70,000**

FUNGI
First appeared
about **1,500 million** years ago.

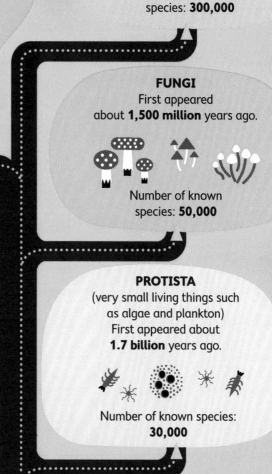

Number of known
species: **50,000**

PROTISTA
(very small living things such
as algae and plankton)
First appeared about
1.7 billion years ago.

Number of known species:
30,000

4 The Earth moves faster...

than anything on Earth.

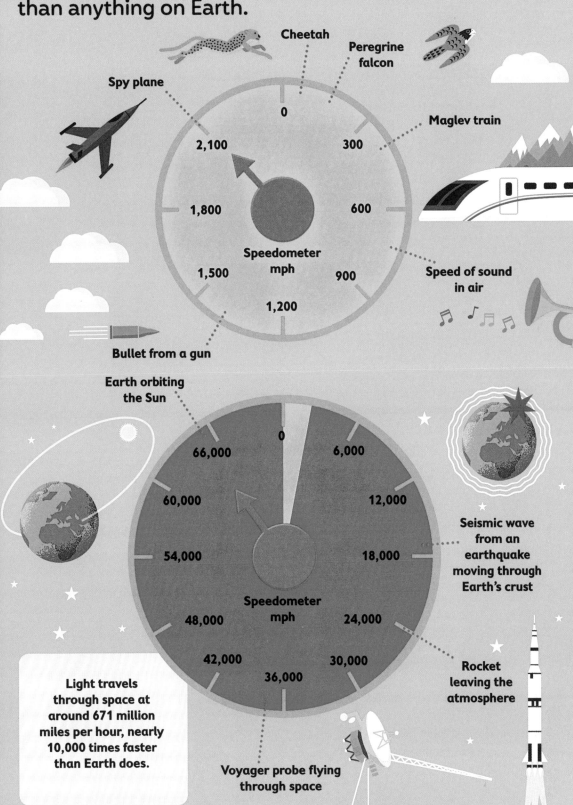

Cheetah

Peregrine falcon

Spy plane

Maglev train

0

2,100   300

1,800   600

Speedometer
mph

1,500   900

Speed of sound
in air

1,200

Bullet from a gun

Earth orbiting
the Sun

0

66,000   6,000

60,000   12,000

54,000   18,000

Seismic wave
from an
earthquake
moving through
Earth's crust

Speedometer
mph

48,000   24,000

42,000   30,000

36,000

Rocket
leaving the
atmosphere

Light travels
through space at
around 671 million
miles per hour, nearly
10,000 times faster
than Earth does.

Voyager probe flying
through space

5 Your body...

is 65% oxygen.

An adult human body is made up of these chemical elements:

Carbon: **18%**

Calcium: **1%**

Hydrogen: **10%**

Nitrogen: **3%**

Phosphorus: **1%**

Oxygen: **65%**

Most of the oxygen and hydrogen in your body is combined together as water.

Other: **2%**

An adult human body is made up of:

Muscles: **650**

Organs: **78**

Bones: **206**

Skin: **20 square feet**

Approximately
7,000,000,000,000,000,000,000,000,000
(7 octillion) atoms

	Female		Male
	35%	Muscles	45%
	27%	Fat	16%
	14%	Bones	15%
	12%	Organs	12%
	7%	Blood	7%
	5%	Other	5%

There are over *ten times* as many bacteria as there are cells in your body. Luckily, most are harmless.

6 Your household waste...

could end up in a new coat.

Recycling is the process of turning old things into new ones, saving energy and preserving Earth's natural resources.

Plastic

Five plastic bottles...

...can be melted down and processed to make enough material to fill a ski jacket.

They can't be made into new bottles because plastic loses quality when it is recycled.

Aluminum

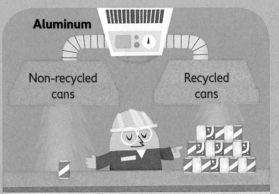

Non-recycled cans

Recycled cans

It takes the same amount of energy to make one non-recycled can as it does to make 20 recycled cans.

Paper

Making paper from scratch uses lots of wood, water and energy. But waste paper can be recycled into new paper. Every ton (900kg) made by recycling waste paper saves:

17 trees

200 bathtubs of water

...and enough energy to power a home for *six months*.

Glass

It takes thousands of years for glass to break down naturally. So if you throw glass bottles away instead of recycling them, they will simply pile up.

Plastic and paper deteriorate each time they are recycled. But glass and aluminum can be recycled over and over again without losing quality.

7 Skyscrapers...
are designed to sway in the wind.

High winds exert a huge force on skyscrapers, making them sway. Engineers must allow for some movement, but make sure buildings won't move more than about 3ft each way or people inside would feel uncomfortable.

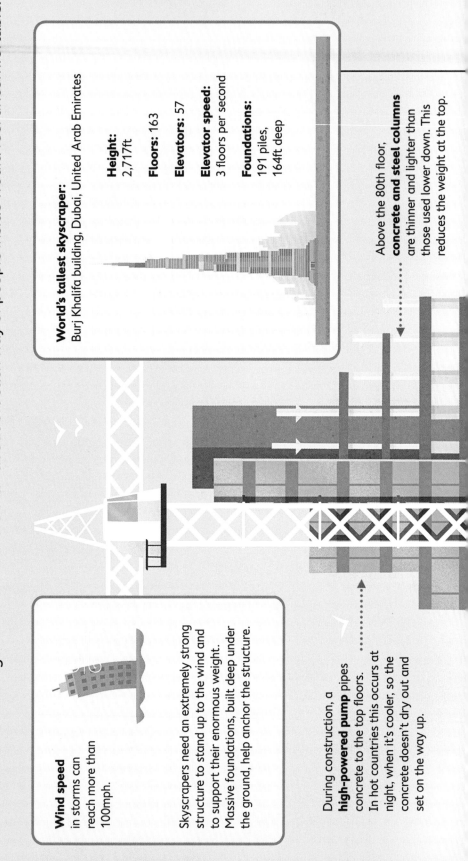

World's tallest skyscraper:
Burj Khalifa building, Dubai, United Arab Emirates

Height:
2,717ft

Floors: 163

Elevators: 57

Elevator speed:
3 floors per second

Foundations:
191 piles,
164ft deep

Above the 80th floor, **concrete and steel columns** are thinner and lighter than those used lower down. This reduces the weight at the top.

Wind speed
in storms can reach more than 100mph.

Skyscrapers need an extremely strong structure to stand up to the wind and to support their enormous weight. Massive foundations, built deep under the ground, help anchor the structure.

During construction, a **high-powered pump** pipes concrete to the top floors. In hot countries this occurs at night, when it's cooler, so the concrete doesn't dry out and set on the way up.

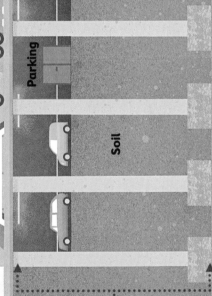

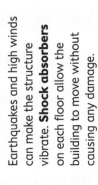

A **thick concrete wall** around the elevators creates a rigid core.

High strength concrete columns, over 3ft thick, carry part of the building's weight.

The **outside wall**, which is made from glass, aluminum and steel, does not carry any of the building's weight.

Piles – steel rods surrounded by concrete

Footing – made of concrete

Hard rock

Parking

Soil

Earthquakes and high winds can make the structure vibrate. **Shock absorbers** on each floor allow the building to move without causing any damage.

Piston

Sticky liquid

The piston moves back and forth in the liquid as the building moves.

Deep foundations carry most of the building's weight and stop it from collapsing or sinking into the ground. They are built on solid rock or a wide concrete base.

8 Without the atmosphere...

we wouldn't survive on Earth.

The atmosphere is a mixture of gases which surrounds the Earth. The outer layers – the thermosphere and the exosphere – merge into space at around 90km (50 miles) up. Here's what happens in the three lower layers.

Mesosphere

Space rocks called **meteors** fall toward Earth, but they break up into dust in the mesosphere. Any small pieces which get through and hit the Earth's surface are called **meteorites**.

Sun's rays

The Sun gives out lots of ultraviolet radiation, which can damage, or even kill, living things.

50km (31 miles)

The Ozone Layer
Within the stratosphere is the Ozone Layer. It contains ozone gas, which absorbs most of the Sun's harmful radiation before it reaches Earth.

Stratosphere

12km (7.5 miles)

Troposphere

This layer is the air that we breathe to stay alive. Weather forms in the troposphere.

Gases in the troposphere trap heat that rises from Earth, stopping it from getting too cold at night.

9 The very first feathers...
weren't used for flying.

The earliest known animals with feathers weren't birds – they were dinosaurs. These dinosaurs couldn't fly, but their feathers probably helped them in lots of other ways:

Staying warm:
Some dinosaurs were covered in long, threadlike feathers that would have been perfect for trapping warm air next to their skin.

Blending in:
Others had feathers with camouflage patterns that helped them to hide from predators – or to ambush prey.

Standing out:
Some species evolved bright, bold feathers to attract mates or warn off possible competitors.

Getting around:
Although they couldn't fly, some dinosaurs probably used their feathered limbs to glide from the treetops.

Getting away:
Feathers could mask a dinosaur's real body shape. This confused would-be predators, and might leave them with nothing more than a mouthful of feathers.

10 If venom gets into your body...

doing nothing can help you get better.

Venom is poison from an animal bite or sting. It spreads quickly through the body in blood, and stops organs from working properly, causing illness or even death.

Common symptoms:

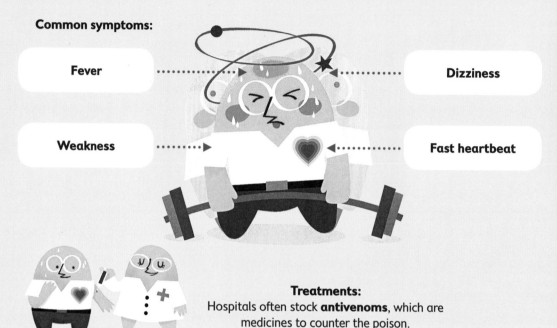

Fever

Dizziness

Weakness

Fast heartbeat

Treatments:
Hospitals often stock **antivenoms**, which are medicines to counter the poison.

If medical help isn't available, there are still ways to increase your chance of survival.

Tie a bandage tightly above the wound.
It will slow the blood flow and stop the poison from spreading.

Lower the wound.
Keeping the wound below your heart will slow the poison from entering your bloodstream.

DO NOTHING.
Panicking or moving around causes blood to flow faster, which makes the poison spread more quickly.

Venom from a **Sydney funnel-web spider bite can kill a person in 15 minutes.**

Actual size

11 The Moon doesn't shine...

it reflects light from the Sun.

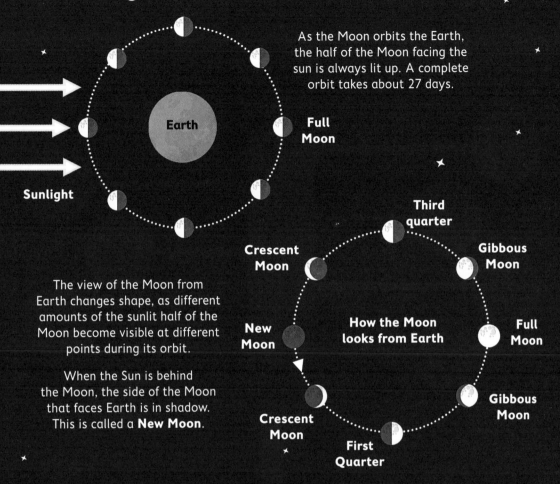

As the Moon orbits the Earth, the half of the Moon facing the sun is always lit up. A complete orbit takes about 27 days.

Sunlight

Earth

Full Moon

The view of the Moon from Earth changes shape, as different amounts of the sunlit half of the Moon become visible at different points during its orbit.

When the Sun is behind the Moon, the side of the Moon that faces Earth is in shadow. This is called a **New Moon**.

Third quarter

Crescent Moon

Gibbous Moon

New Moon

How the Moon looks from Earth

Full Moon

Crescent Moon

First Quarter

Gibbous Moon

On a **Full Moon**, the half that we can see is fully lit. Even then, the Moon only reflects **12%** of the light that shines on it because its surface is so bumpy.

Craters – holes made by lumps of rock that have hit the surface

Lunar highlands – higher areas, lighter shades of rock

Dry, powdery surface, scattered with rocks

Maria – low, flat areas of dark volcanic rock

Full Moon

12 Acid in your stomach...

is ten times stronger than vinegar.

When dissolved in water, all substances are **acids**, **bases** or **neutral**. They can be measured on the pH scale (pH stands for 'power of hydrogen'). It runs from very strong base (pH14) to very strong acid (pH0). The scale below shows the strength of some common substances.

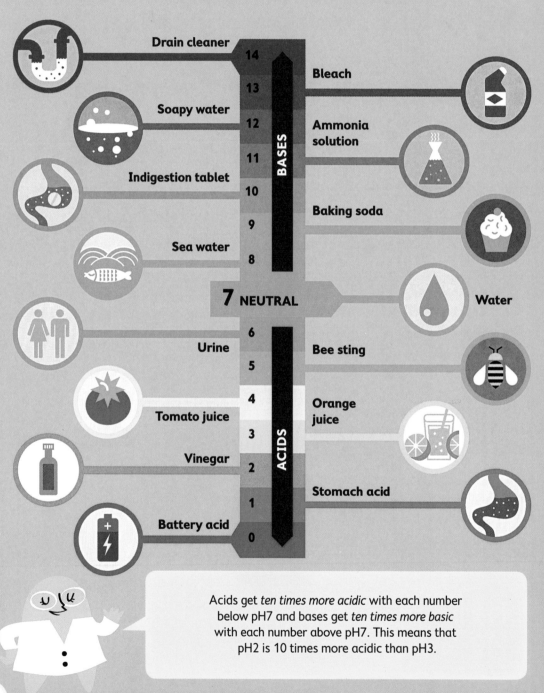

Acids get *ten times more acidic* with each number below pH7 and bases get *ten times more basic* with each number above pH7. This means that pH2 is 10 times more acidic than pH3.

13 Streamlined shapes...

can slice through air and water.

A kingfisher's beak is smooth and wedge-shaped. This is known as a streamlined shape.

A flat-shaped beak has a bigger surface area. It uses lots of energy to push against the water, creating a big splash.

A streamlined wedge shape cuts through water at high speed with little resistance, so it uses less energy.

In 1997 Japanese engineers copied the shape of a kingfisher's beak to design a high speed *Shinkansen* (bullet) train.

Its streamlined shape cuts through air more smoothly than flatter-nosed trains, so it uses less energy and fuel. It also makes less noise.

Air flow

High-speed trains push against the air in a tunnel. As the air escapes the tunnel, it rapidly expands, which can cause a loud boom.

But the streamlined design of the bullet train reduces air resistance dramatically, so there is no boom.

look back in time.

Large Magellanic Cloud
(brightest galaxy)
163,000 years ago

Canis Major Dwarf Galaxy
(nearest galaxy to ours)
25,000 years ago

Telescopes can detect
light from distant objects
such as stars
and galaxies.

Because light takes time
to travel long distances,
we actually see things the
way they looked in the
past — at the time when
the light started traveling
from them to us.

Deneb
(blue supergiant)
1,550 years ago

Polaris
(the North Star)
430 years ago

Sirius
(brightest visible star)
8.6 years ago

Some of the stars
we see today may
already have burned
out — but we won't
know for many
years to come.

Pluto
(at its nearest point)
4 hours ago

Proxima Centauri
(nearest star after the Sun)
4.3 years ago

Jupiter
(at its nearest point)
33 minutes ago

15 Fireworks...

are 1,000,000,000 times louder than talking.

Noise is measured in decibels (dB). Each 10dB is 10 times louder than the last. So 30dB is 10 times louder than 20dB, and 100 times louder than 10dB.

Rustling leaves

20dB

TV
70dB

Talking
60dB

0dB	Weakest sound possible
10dB	Breathing
20dB	Rustling leaves
30dB	Whispering
40dB	Tweeting birds
50dB	Refrigerator
60dB	Talking
70dB	TV
80dB	Truck
90dB	Hairdryer
100dB	Drum roll
110dB	Trombone
120dB	Police siren
130dB	Power drill
140dB	Military jet plane
150dB	Fireworks

Truck
80dB

Trombone
110dB

Military jet plane
140dB

Fireworks
150dB

16 Carl Linnaeus...

gave human beings their scientific name.

Swedish botanist and zoologist Carl Linnaeus was fascinated by plants and animals. He came up with the system for naming and classifying species – including humans – that is used today.

1707
Carl Linnaeus was born in Småland, Sweden.

1717
As a boy, Carl often skipped school to hunt for plants.

1732
On an expedition to Lapland, he found a new plant that is now named after him: *Linnea borealis*. During his career, he made many such expeditions and found hundreds of unnamed species.

Here's how Linnaeus classified *himself* (and all other humans):

Kingdom: *Animalis*
Class: *Mammalia*
Order: *Primate*
Genus: *Homo*
Species: *sapiens*

...or *Homo sapiens* for short.

1735
His book, *Systema Naturae*, divided living things into logical categories, and used a new way of naming species with just two Latin names.

1758
The 10th edition of *Systema Naturae* first grouped whales with mammals, and apes with humans.

1760s
He sent his students all over the world to document new plant and animal species.

Died: 1778
In his later years, Carl Linnaeus was made a nobleman by the King of Sweden.

17 Apes and monkeys...

are our closest relatives.

Humans, apes and monkeys are all **mammals**, in the order known as **primates**.

Capuchin monkey
Cebus capucinus

Howler monkey
Alouatta guariba

Spider monkey
Ateles fusciceps

Macaque
Macaca sylvanus

Squirrel monkey
Saimiri sciureus

Proboscis monkey
Nasalis larvatus

Chimpanzee
Pan troglodytes

Primates all share certain characteristics that set them apart from other mammals:

· excellent eyesight
· reduced sense of smell
· large brains
· bodies that are adapted for climbing trees

Humans, gorillas, chimpanzees and orangutans are all **great apes**. They are larger and brainier than monkeys.

Mandrill
Mandrillus sphinx

Orangutan
Pongo abelii

Gorilla
Gorilla gorilla

Human
Homo sapiens

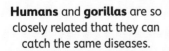

Humans and **gorillas** are so closely related that they can catch the same diseases.

In zoos, vets give gorilla babies many of the same vaccinations that human babies get.

18 Cars...

can run on coconuts.

Most cars are powered by a fossil fuel called gasoline.
But scientists are developing alternatives.

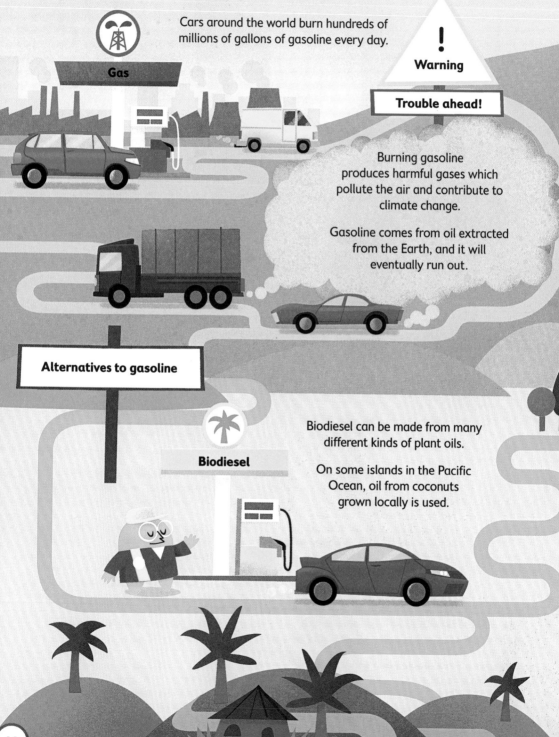

Cars around the world burn hundreds of millions of gallons of gasoline every day.

Gas

!
Warning

Trouble ahead!

Burning gasoline produces harmful gases which pollute the air and contribute to climate change.

Gasoline comes from oil extracted from the Earth, and it will eventually run out.

Alternatives to gasoline

Biodiesel

Biodiesel can be made from many different kinds of plant oils.

On some islands in the Pacific Ocean, oil from coconuts grown locally is used.

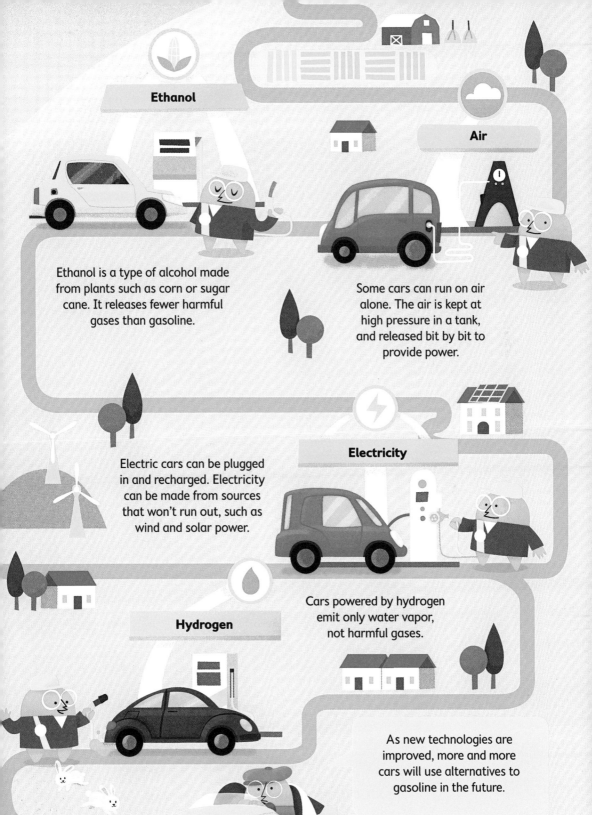

Ethanol

Ethanol is a type of alcohol made from plants such as corn or sugar cane. It releases fewer harmful gases than gasoline.

Air

Some cars can run on air alone. The air is kept at high pressure in a tank, and released bit by bit to provide power.

Electricity

Electric cars can be plugged in and recharged. Electricity can be made from sources that won't run out, such as wind and solar power.

Hydrogen

Cars powered by hydrogen emit only water vapor, not harmful gases.

As new technologies are improved, more and more cars will use alternatives to gasoline in the future.

23

19 The Earth's surface...

is mostly water.

Water covers **71%** of the globe. Land covers only **29%**.

This diagram shows approximately how much of the Earth's surface
is covered by various types of terrain.

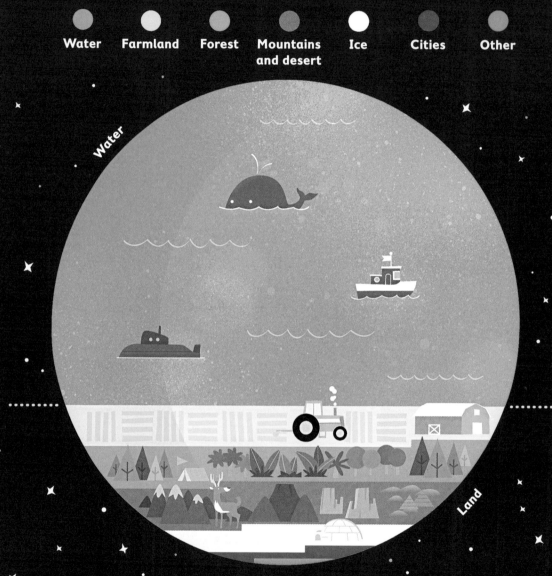

Water   Farmland   Forest   Mountains   Ice   Cities   Other
and desert

What will the Earth look like in 50 years?
Earth's population is growing by about **80 million people** each year. This means we will
need more and more living space and farmland. Human activity is also heating up the
planet, melting ice and raising sea levels. So, in the future, there will be
even more ocean and *even less land*.

20 Almost two-thirds of all moths...

are still unknown to science.

Moths inhabit every continent except Antarctica. Scientists estimate there may be up to **400,000** species worldwide – but only **150,000** have been identified so far. Here are a few of them.

Attacus atlas

The **biggest moth** has a wingspan of over 10in and wingtips that look like snakes' heads.

Cryptoses choloepi

Sloth moths live only in the fur of sloths, and they lay their eggs in sloth dung.

Uropyia meticulodina

Many moths are masters of disguise. This one looks like a **dead leaf**.

Acontia aprica

Some moths have evolved to look like **bird droppings** to discourage predators.

Acherontia atropos

Death's-head hawkmoths look and smell a lot like bees, and can sneak into hives to steal honey.

Actias luna

Luna moths don't have mouths, and don't eat or drink during their adult lives.

21 Extinctions...

happen all the time.

A species becomes extinct when its last individual member dies. This diagram shows just some of the extinctions we know about from recent history.

Number of species lost:

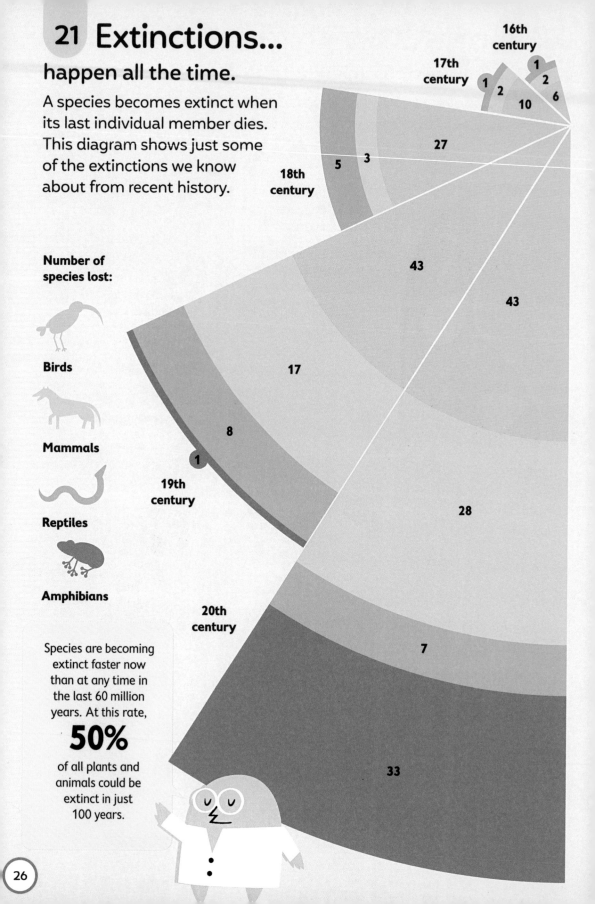

Birds

Mammals

Reptiles

Amphibians

16th century

17th century

18th century

19th century

20th century

1
2
6
1
2
10
27
5
3
43
43
17
8
1
28
7
33

Species are becoming extinct faster now than at any time in the last 60 million years. At this rate,

50%

of all plants and animals could be extinct in just 100 years.

26

Why do species become extinct?
Extinctions are often caused by several overlapping factors.
This diagram shows some of the most common.

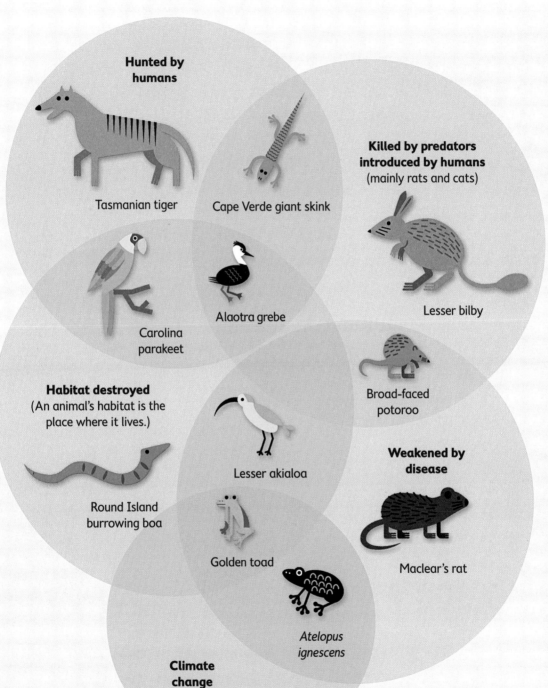

Hunted by humans

Tasmanian tiger

Cape Verde giant skink

Killed by predators introduced by humans
(mainly rats and cats)

Lesser bilby

Carolina parakeet

Alaotra grebe

Broad-faced potoroo

Habitat destroyed
(An animal's habitat is the place where it lives.)

Lesser akialoa

Weakened by disease

Round Island burrowing boa

Golden toad

Maclear's rat

Atelopus ignescens

Climate change

22 The Earth...

is not entirely solid.

Deep below the hard surface where we live, the Earth is made up of layers, including hot molten rock and liquid metal.

Continental crust
makes up the land.

The Earth's crust
is a thin layer of solid rock.
There are two types.

Oceanic crust
makes up the
ocean floors.

The crust and upper mantle sit on top
of a layer of rock which flows very slowly.

Mantle
Mostly solid rock, with small,
very hot molten parts.

Rock near the
scorching hot core
heats up and rises.

Cooler rock from the
surface sinks.

In the inner core,
temperatures reach

10,800°F
(6,000°C).

Only extremely high
pressure stops it
from melting.

Outer core
A layer of flowing
liquid metal.

The center of the
Earth is **3,954 miles**
below the surface.

Inner core
A ball of
solid metal.

23 Tsunami...
can be as tall as skyscrapers.

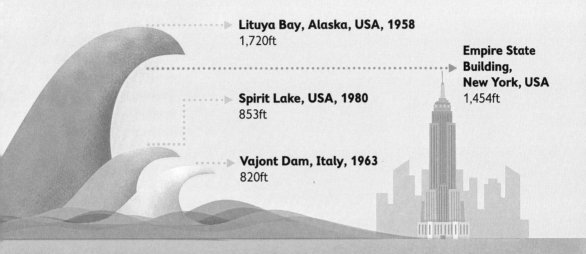

Lituya Bay, Alaska, USA, 1958
1,720ft

Empire State Building, New York, USA
1,454ft

Spirit Lake, USA, 1980
853ft

Vajont Dam, Italy, 1963
820ft

Tsunami are powerful waves often caused by earthquakes or volcanic eruptions deep under the ocean.

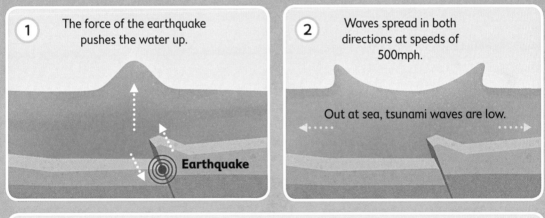

1 The force of the earthquake pushes the water up.

Earthquake

2 Waves spread in both directions at speeds of 500mph.

Out at sea, tsunami waves are low.

3 As the waves reach shallow water, they slow down and increase in height.

Five minutes before some tsunami hit the shore, sea water may suddenly draw back for over 3,000ft. Warning systems are designed to spot this type of unusual wave activity, so beaches can be evacuated.

24 Marie Curie...

was killed by her own discovery.

French–Polish scientist Marie Curie studied new radioactive elements and came up with a theory of radioactivity.

1867
Marie Curie was born in Warsaw, Poland.

1898
Marie and her husband Pierre discovered the elements **radium** and **polonium**.

1903 and 1911
Marie was the first woman to win a Nobel Prize. In fact, she won two: one in physics and one in chemistry.

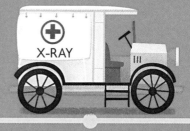

Unaware of the dangers of radiation, Marie used to carry around radioactive material in her pockets.

1914–1918
During the First World War, Marie developed mobile X-ray labs to help doctors working on the front lines.

1934
After years of exposure to materials such as radium and uranium, Marie died of radiation poisoning.

Today, Marie Curie's books and papers are still too radioactive to handle without protective equipment.

25 Phosphorus...

is flammable, poisonous – and essential to life.

On its own, the element phosphorus can be extremely dangerous. But, when combined with other elements, it creates many of the safe, useful chemicals found in living cells.

Pure white phosphorus glows in the dark.

If exposed to oxygen, it bursts into flame.

Eating just a speck of pure phosphorus can put a person in a coma.

Touching pure phosphorus can cause serious burns.

Phosphorus is the 6th most common element in the human body.

We eat it every day in foods such as meat and grains.

Phosphorus helps bones and teeth grow properly.

Phosphorus is used in plant food, matches, and detergents.

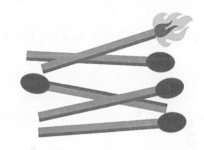

Phosphorus was discovered by the German experimenter **Hennig Brand** in 1669. The discovery was an accident. He had actually been trying to turn urine into gold.

The substance Hennig discovered glowed in the dark. He decided to name it phosphorus from the Greek word *phosphoros* which means "bringer of light."

Stars burn and change...

over a lifetime that lasts for billions of years.

Stage 1: birth

A star begins life as a vast cloud of gas and space dust called a **nebula**. Over millions of years, it gradually clusters together.

Stage 2: ball of fire

As the nebula clusters, it forms a ball that begins to burn, becoming something called a **main sequence star**. The bigger the ball, the brighter it burns.

Medium-sized stars glow orange or yellow, and burn for billions of years.

The Sun is a medium size main sequence star.

Stage 3: cooling off

Eventually, stars begin to cool down, expand and glow deep red for up to a billion years. These are called **red giants**.

The biggest stars glow green or blue. Some burn out in just a few million years.

The biggest stars **expand so much** they are known as **red supergiants.**

Stage 4: remnant

A red giant slowly boils away, leaving behind a planet-sized glowing ball called a **white dwarf**.

Astronomers believe that white dwarfs eventually cool completely, becoming **black dwarfs**.

So far, no one has ever found a black dwarf, and it's possible that none actually exist – yet.

Sudden death!

Sometimes, massive stars can blow up long before they burn out, creating a short-lived but amazingly bright explosion called a **supernova**. The explosion leaves behind one of two long-lasting **remnants**:

A **supernova** burns for just a few years.

1 An incredibly hot, dense ball called a **neutron star**.

2 An object so dense and powerful, not even light can escape it. This is known as a **black hole**.

The dust and gas flung out by a supernova gradually comes together as a new **nebula**.

27 Scientists expect alien life...

to be found in the Goldilocks zone.

The planets most likely to support life orbit in what astronomers call the **Goldilocks zone**. This is an area not too near and not too far from a star.

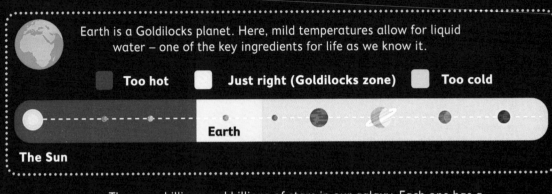

Earth is a Goldilocks planet. Here, mild temperatures allow for liquid water – one of the key ingredients for life as we know it.

◼ Too hot   ◻ Just right (Goldilocks zone)   ◻ Too cold

Earth

The Sun

There are billions and billions of stars in our galaxy. Each one has a Goldilocks zone. The cooler the star is, the closer its zone will be.

A red dwarf
(cool and dim)

Goldilocks planets

A blue giant
(hot and bright)

Other Goldilocks planets, orbiting other stars, may be good places to look for alien life.

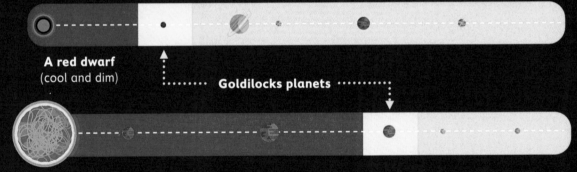

View of an imagined Goldilocks planet

So far, astronomers have found about **40** Goldilocks planets. They think there may be **40 billion** more in our galaxy.

Mild temperatures

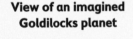

Liquid seas

Forests

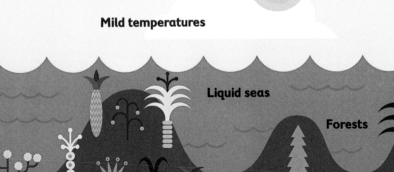

28 Tiny underwater plants...

can change the weather.

Phytoplankton are microscopic, floating plants that live in the upper layers of oceans and lakes. They may be tiny, but they have a big impact on the weather.

Phytoplankton need sunlight to survive – but too much sun can harm them. So, they've developed a way of *creating their own shade.*

1

Phytoplankton react to intense sunlight by producing a chemical.

2

This chemical breaks down and evaporates into the air, where it forms dust-like particles.

3

In moist air, billions of water droplets condense around the particles, creating a cloud.

4

This makes some cooling shade for the phytoplankton down below.

Phytoplankton

29 The largest living organism...

is a fungus.

It is called *Armillaria solidipes*, and it feeds on the wood and roots of trees.

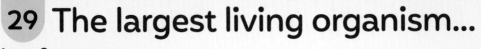

The fungus has delicate, root-like threads that grow under bark and through the forest floor. Over thousands of years, they can form a vast network, known as a **colony**.

One colony in Oregon, in the USA, is known as the **Humongous Fungus**. It covers an area of 3.5 square miles. That's about the same as 7,200 Olympic-size swimming pools.

The largest animals
(Shown to scale)

Largest animal:
Blue whale
Balaenoptera musculus
84 feet long

Largest reptile:
Saltwater crocodile
Crocodylus porosus
17 feet long

Largest land animal:
African bush elephant
Loxodonta africana
11 feet tall

30 The smallest living organism...

is almost invisible – even under a microscope.

The organism is called the **Archaeal Richmond Mine acidophilic nano-organism**, or ARMAN. It was first found in hot, highly acidic water in an old copper mine.

These creatures are so small, you could fit **100,000** of them in a single grain of table salt.

More of the smallest animals
(Shown at actual size)

Smallest primate:
Mouse lemur from Madagascar
Microcebus berthae
8.3 inches long

Smallest bird:
Bee hummingbird from Cuba
Mellisuga helenae
2 inches long

Smallest fish:
Cyprinid from Indonesia
Paedocypris progenetica
0.4 inches long

Smallest reptile:
Chameleon from Madagascar
Brookesia micra
1 inch long

Smallest amphibian:
Frog from Papua New Guinea
Paedophryne amauensis
0.3 inches long

31 Oil underground comes from...

animals and plants that lived millions of years ago.

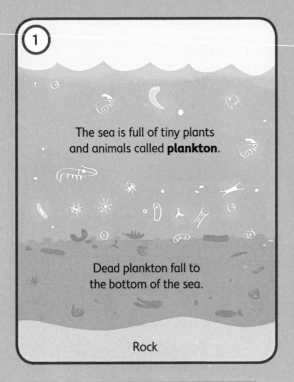

1

The sea is full of tiny plants and animals called **plankton**.

Dead plankton fall to the bottom of the sea.

Rock

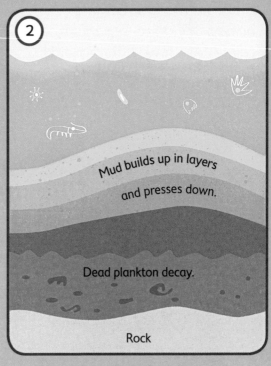

2

Mud builds up in layers and presses down.

Dead plankton decay.

Rock

3

Over millions of years...

High pressure and heat turn the mud into rock...

and the decayed plankton into oil.

Oil

Rock

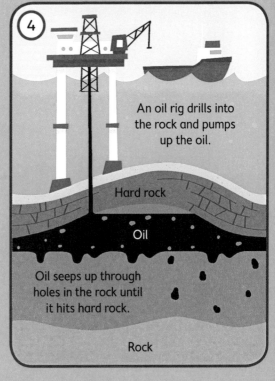

4

An oil rig drills into the rock and pumps up the oil.

Hard rock

Oil

Oil seeps up through holes in the rock until it hits hard rock.

Rock

Oil is taken to an oil refinery.
It is heated to make it separate into parts in a **distillation tower**.
Each part can be used for many different products – from plastic and fuel to paint and perfume.

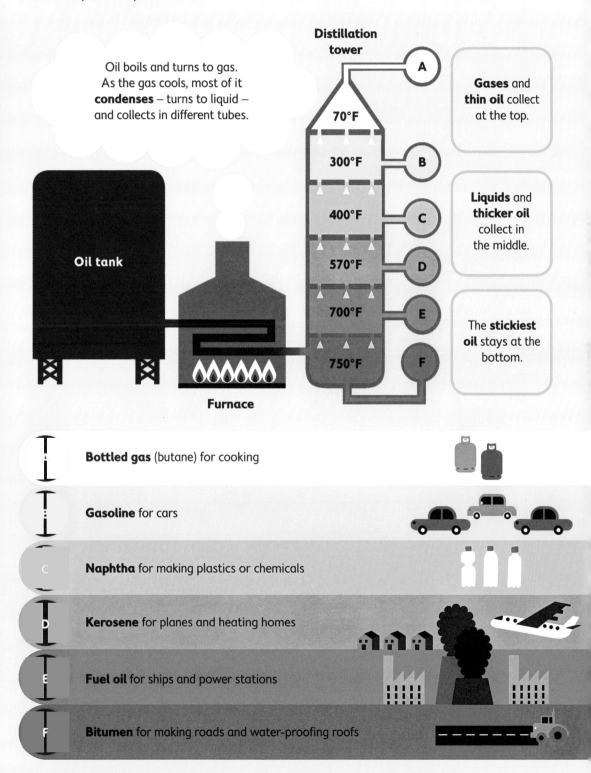

Oil boils and turns to gas. As the gas cools, most of it **condenses** – turns to liquid – and collects in different tubes.

Distillation tower

A

70°F

300°F — B

400°F — C

570°F — D

700°F — E

750°F — F

Gases and **thin oil** collect at the top.

Liquids and **thicker oil** collect in the middle.

The **stickiest oil** stays at the bottom.

Oil tank

Furnace

A — **Bottled gas** (butane) for cooking

B — **Gasoline** for cars

C — **Naphtha** for making plastics or chemicals

D — **Kerosene** for planes and heating homes

E — **Fuel oil** for ships and power stations

F — **Bitumen** for making roads and water-proofing roofs

32 The Earth has two North Poles...

and two South Poles.

The Earth has **geographic poles** and **magnetic poles** – but they're not in the same place.

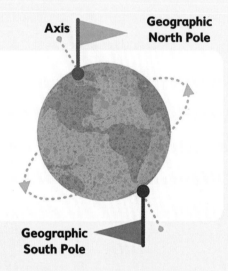

Axis

Geographic North Pole

Geographic poles

The Earth rotates around an invisible line called an axis. The **geographic poles** are the two points where the axis passes through the planet's surface.

Geographic South Pole

Magnetic North Pole

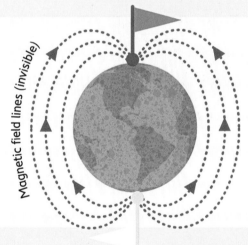

Magnetic field lines (invisible)

Magnetic poles

There is a layer of liquid metal swirling around the Earth's core. It creates a powerful, invisible magnetic field which surrounds the entire planet.

The places where this field points straight down into – or straight up out of – the ground are called the **magnetic poles**.

Magnetic South Pole

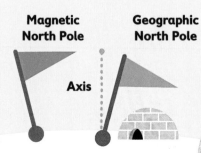

Magnetic North Pole

Geographic North Pole

Magnetic compasses aim toward the Magnetic North Pole.

Axis

Today, the geographic and magnetic North Poles are roughly **285 miles** apart. But the distance is changing all the time.

33 The Earth's magnetic poles...

are constantly moving.

The magnetic poles don't have fixed positions. Because of unpredictable changes in the planet's core, they drift across the Earth's surface.

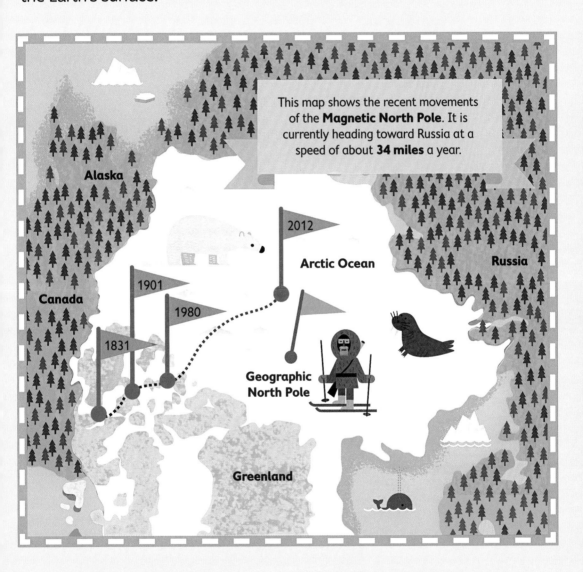

This map shows the recent movements of the **Magnetic North Pole**. It is currently heading toward Russia at a speed of about **34 miles** a year.

Alaska

2012

Arctic Ocean

Russia

1901

Canada

1980

1831

Geographic North Pole

Greenland

Sometimes – for reasons scientists don't fully understand – the Earth's magnetic field *flips*, so that it flows from north to south (instead of flowing south to north as it does now).

Scientists studying magnetic traces in rocks on the ocean floor have discovered that this has happened as many as **12 times** in the last 3 million years.

34 Bridges can span...

up to 1.2 miles between supports.

Huge forces push and pull on bridges. Designs that balance out these forces best span the greatest distances.

Compression (pushing force) →←

Tension (pulling force) ←→

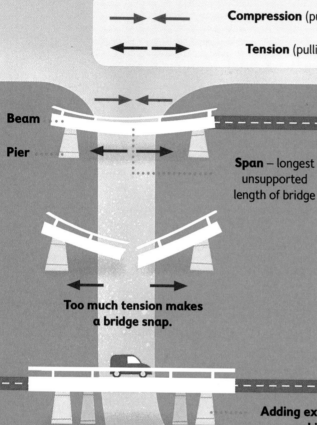

Beam

Pier

Span – longest unsupported length of bridge

Too much tension makes a bridge snap.

Beam bridge

This is the most basic kind of bridge. It consists of a horizontal beam with supports, or piers, at each end.

Span: up to 250 feet

Adding extra piers spreads the forces, making the bridge stronger.

Arch bridge

This semicircular shape spreads the compression force and transfers the weight to supports at each end.

Span: up to 1,800 feet

Truss bridge

This bridge uses a structure called a truss, made up of triangular sections. This spreads the forces over a wide area, strengthening the design.

Span: up to 1,300 feet

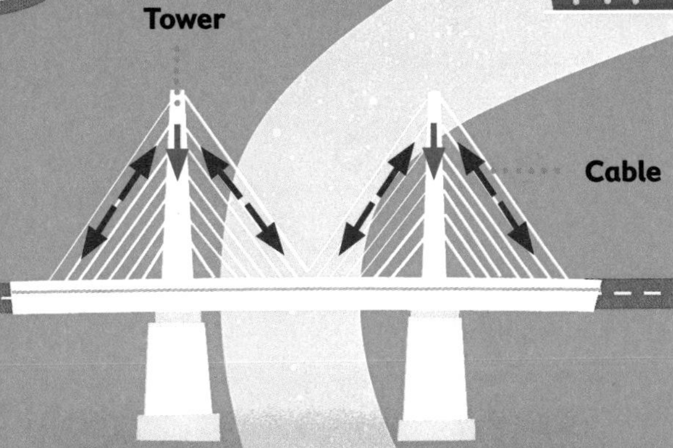

Tower

Cable

Cable-stayed bridge

Steel cables span from the main roadway up to one or more towers, which carry the load.

Span: up to 3,000 feet

Tower

Cables

Suspension bridge

Steel cables transfer most of the forces to two towers. This bridge style is more expensive to build but can span the longest distance.

Span: up to 1.2 miles (6,500 feet)

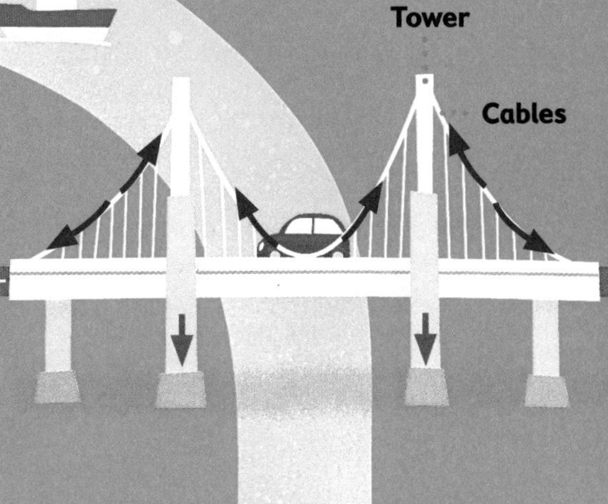

35 Lightning is five times hotter...

than the surface of the Sun.

Lightning is a form of static electricity that's made in storm clouds.

1

Clouds are made of:

Water droplets...   ...ice crystals...   ...and hailstones.

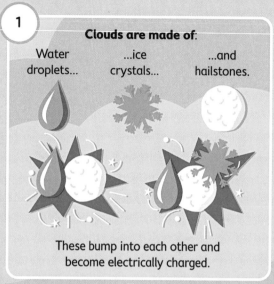

These bump into each other and become electrically charged.

2

Hailstones pick up negative charged particles and fall to the lower part of the cloud.

Negative charge

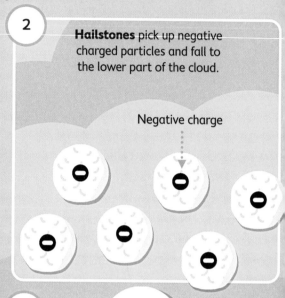

3

The negative charges in the lower part of the cloud and positive charges on the ground are attracted to each other.

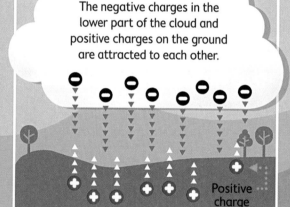

Positive charge

4

The charges meet, causing a massive flow of electricity. This is **lightning**.

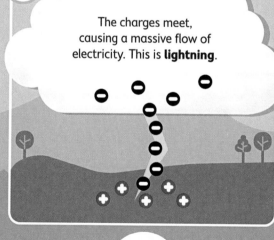

Electric current flows down to Earth at up to **30 million miles per hour**. In a flash, lightning can reach **54,000°F (30,000°C)**.

Lightning can make the moisture inside a tree boil instantly, causing the tree to explode.

The temperature on the surface of the Sun is 10,000–11,000°F (5,500–6,000°C).

36 Dung beetles use the Milky Way...
to find their way around.

When a dung beetle finds fresh dung to eat, it packs a portion into a ball and rolls it away from any lurking predators or competitors.

The Milky Way

During the day, the beetle uses the position of the sun to steer in a straight line.

At night, it sets a course using the glowing band of stars that form the heart of the **Milky Way galaxy**.

37 Most of the universe...
is made of stuff that is impossible to detect.

Most scientists agree that the universe is made up of three basic types of stuff:

1

Atomic matter (less than 5% of the universe) is what stars, planets and people are made of.

2

Dark matter (around 27% of the universe) is invisible, barely detectable matter that helps hold galaxies together.

3

Dark energy is everything else

The only thing anyone knows about so-called **dark energy** is that it's making the universe expand

38 Volcanic eruptions...

happen because the Earth melts its own crust.

An eruption is an explosion of liquid rock and hot gases escaping from beneath the Earth's crust.

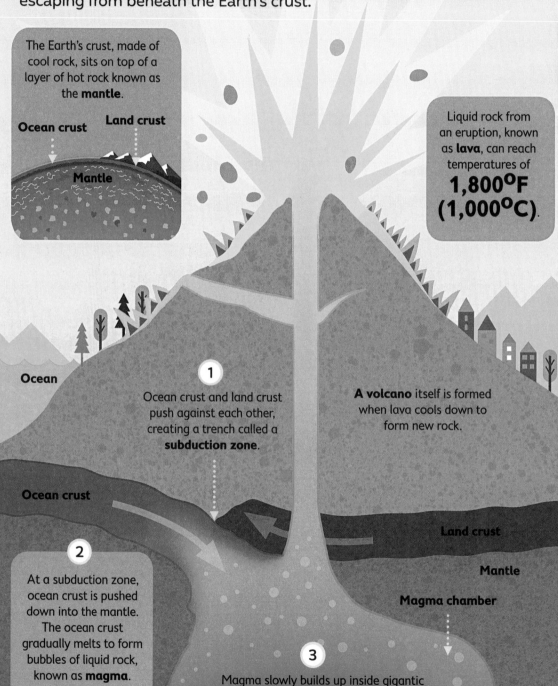

The Earth's crust, made of cool rock, sits on top of a layer of hot rock known as the **mantle**.

Ocean crust **Land crust**

Mantle

Liquid rock from an eruption, known as **lava**, can reach temperatures of

1,800°F (1,000°C).

Ocean

1

Ocean crust and land crust push against each other, creating a trench called a **subduction zone**.

A volcano itself is formed when lava cools down to form new rock.

Ocean crust

Land crust

Mantle

2

At a subduction zone, ocean crust is pushed down into the mantle. The ocean crust gradually melts to form bubbles of liquid rock, known as **magma**.

Magma chamber

3

Magma slowly builds up inside gigantic underground wells called **magma chambers**. In time, these become so full that they explode out of the ground.

39 An eruption in Indonesia...

caused a major famine in Europe.

1815 saw the biggest volcanic eruption in recorded history – Mount Tambora in Indonesia. It was the fourth major eruption in the region in four years.

In the days that followed Mount Tambora's eruption, people across Indonesia died in a deluge of fire and hot ash.

North America

Europe

Suwanosejima, Japan 1813

Mayon volcano, Philippines 1814

Mt. Awu, Indonesia 1812

Africa

Mt. Tambora, Indonesia 1815

Over the months following the Tambora eruption, a vast cloud of ash spread across the northern hemisphere, bringing storms and bad weather.

The cloud blocked sunlight for months, resulting in widespread crop failure.

Deaths directly caused by the eruption:	Indonesia: 10,000 Europe: 0
Deaths caused by crop failure and other environmental effects:	Indonesia: 71,000 Europe: 200,000

1816 became known as 'The year without a summer'.

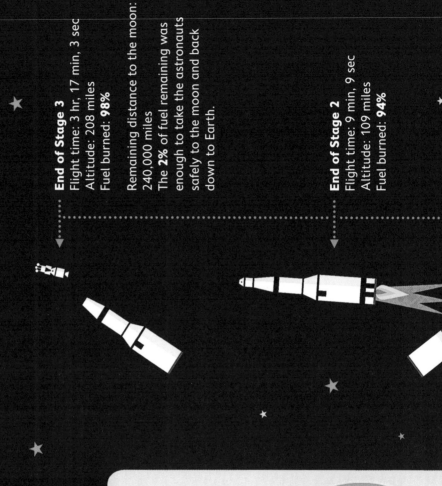

Most space rockets...

burn three quarters of their fuel in the first three minutes of flight.

It takes a huge amount of energy to lift a rocket into orbit. To get the push they
need to overcome Earth's gravity, rockets burn vast quantities of explosive fuel.

End of Stage 3
Flight time: 3 hr, 17 min, 3 sec
Altitude: 208 miles
Fuel burned: **98%**

Remaining distance to the moon:
240,000 miles
The **2%** of fuel remaining was
enough to take the astronauts
safely to the moon and back
down to Earth.

End of Stage 2
Flight time: 9 min, 9 sec
Altitude: 109 miles
Fuel burned: **94%**

In 1969, the **Apollo 11**
mission put the first men
on the moon. The rocket
weighed **6.5 million lbs.**
Most of this was fuel.

Fuel
93%
of total
weight

7% **Other
stuff**

Outer space   **Atmosphere**

100km   **62 miles**

End of Stage 1
Flight time: 2 min, 42 sec
Altitude: 42 miles
Fuel burned: **77%**

Takeoff
Rocket loaded with about
6 million lbs of fuel.

In less than **three minutes,**
the rocket burned about
4.7 million lbs of fuel.

That's roughly what a 747
Jumbo Jet would use to fly
around the Earth **four times.**

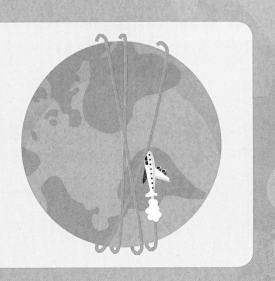

41 Everything you can see...

is made of billions upon *billions* of atoms.

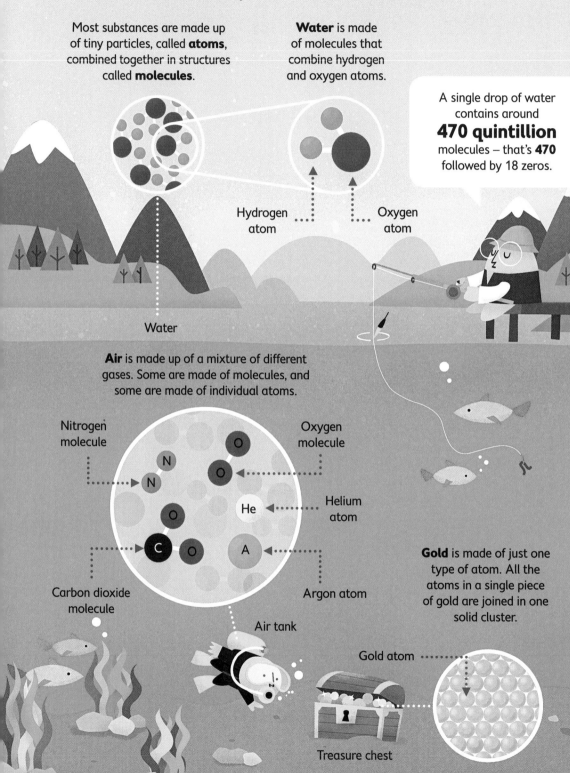

Most substances are made up of tiny particles, called **atoms**, combined together in structures called **molecules**.

Water is made of molecules that combine hydrogen and oxygen atoms.

A single drop of water contains around **470 quintillion** molecules – that's **470** followed by 18 zeros.

Hydrogen atom

Oxygen atom

Water

Air is made up of a mixture of different gases. Some are made of molecules, and some are made of individual atoms.

Nitrogen molecule

Oxygen molecule

N

N

O

O

O

He

Helium atom

C

O

A

Argon atom

Carbon dioxide molecule

Air tank

Gold is made of just one type of atom. All the atoms in a single piece of gold are joined in one solid cluster.

Gold atom

Treasure chest

42 Atoms are so tiny...

it's impossible to get a good look at them.

Scientists can study an object's atomic structure using a machine called an **electron microscope**.

A computer creates images of what an electron microscope detects.

Magnification: 100 million x actual size

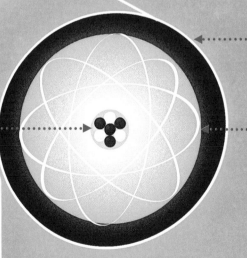

What the screen *can* show: a cluster of atoms.

By breaking atoms apart, scientists have discovered they are made up of even smaller pieces.

What the screen *can't* show: inside an individual atom.

The middle contains a cluster of particles called the **nucleus**.

Electron microscopes can show how atoms are arranged inside a material, and can even show the rough location of individual atoms.

Miniscule particles, called **electrons**, zoom around the nucleus in a cloud.

Even in a solid substance, atoms are constantly jiggling around. Scientists can determine how fast they are moving, or pinpoint their position — but it's impossible to measure both, precisely, at the same time.

43 Vast periods of history...

are measured on a scale known as *deep time*.

1. Timeline of the universe

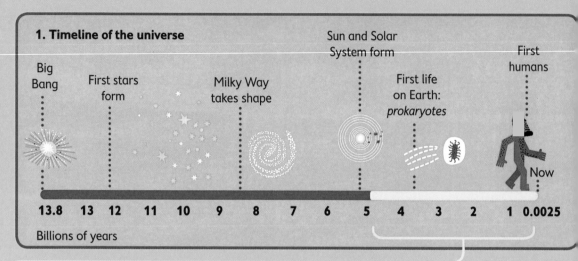

Big Bang

First stars form

Milky Way takes shape

Sun and Solar System form

First life on Earth: *prokaryotes*

First humans

Now

| 13.8 | 13 | 12 | 11 | 10 | 9 | 8 | 7 | 6 | 5 | 4 | 3 | 2 | 1 | 0.0025 |

Billions of years

2. Timeline of planet Earth

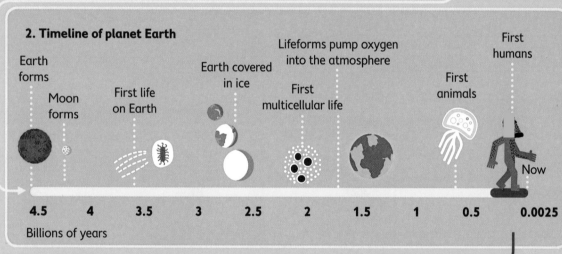

Earth forms

Moon forms

First life on Earth

Earth covered in ice

Lifeforms pump oxygen into the atmosphere

First multicellular life

First animals

First humans

Now

| 4.5 | 4 | 3.5 | 3 | 2.5 | 2 | 1.5 | 1 | 0.5 | 0.0025 |

Billions of years

3. Timeline of human beings

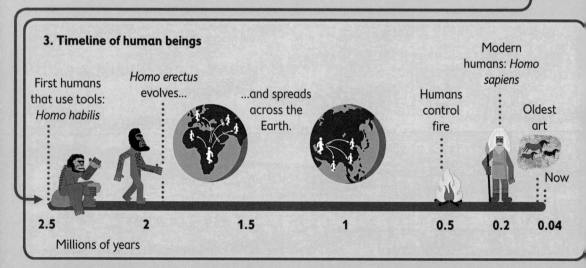

First humans that use tools: *Homo habilis*

Homo erectus evolves...

...and spreads across the Earth.

Humans control fire

Modern humans: *Homo sapiens*

Oldest art

Now

| 2.5 | 2 | 1.5 | 1 | 0.5 | 0.2 | 0.04 |

Millions of years

44 The oldest living animal...
could potentially live forever.

When it gets injured or grows old, the tiny jellyfish *Turritopsis dohrnii* doesn't die. Instead, it reverses the aging process and starts again.

Old jellyfish

Polyp

Clones

1. The old jellyfish sinks to the sea floor.

2. It changes back into a **polyp** (an early stage of jellyfish life).

3. New baby jellyfish grow out of the polyp.

4. These are **clones** (identical copies) of the original creature.

Because it can start life over and over again, *Turritopsis dohrnii* is effectively immortal.

Other organisms use cloning to extend their lifespans, too.

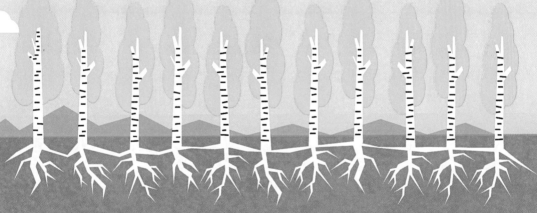

In the US, there is a colony of more than 40,000 quaking aspens known as the **Trembling Giant**.

The trees are all *identical clones*, linked together by a single gigantic root system.

Forest fires can destroy the trees above ground – but afterwards, new clones sprout from the buried roots. The colony's root system is thought to be at least **80,000 years old**.

45 Simple machines...

make difficult tasks easy.

In the 17th century, scientists came up with the idea that six simple machines form the basis for *all* machines. These simple machines work by reducing the force, or effort, you need to complete a task.

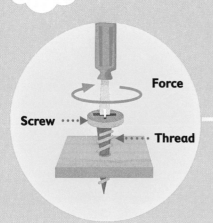

Force

Screw ·····

····· Thread

A **SCREW** has a raised thread wrapped around it. When you turn the screw, the thread cuts into a material. This mechanism can also be used to hold objects in place.

Uses: screw, drill, lightbulb, jar lid

A **WEDGE** can be used to cut things or hold them in place. The sharper the wedge, the easier it cuts.

Examples: ax, knife, teeth, fork, nail, door stopper

Force

An ax is a type of wedge.

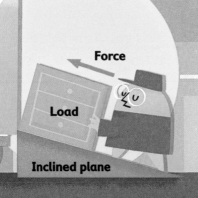

Force

Load

Inclined plane

An **INCLINED PLANE** is a slope that makes it easier to raise a load. The gentler the slope, the less force is needed, but the further you need to move the load.

Examples: ramp, zig-zag path up hill

Adding **extra wheels** to a pulley reduces the amount of downward force a person needs to pull up a load.

Wheel

Force

Rope

A **PULLEY** is a rope wrapped around one or more wheels which is used to lift or pull a load.

Uses: loading pulley, crane, window blind, flag pole

Load

A **WHEEL AND AXLE** is a wheel connected to a rod, or axle, to move a load. The larger the wheel, the easier it is to turn, but the further you have to turn it.

Uses: car, bicycle, wheelbarrow

A **LEVER** is a rod that turns on a pivot or fixed point. Moving the pivot closer to the load makes it easier to lift.

Uses: door handle, scissors, shovel, nut cracker

Wheel

Axle

Force

Load

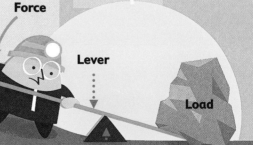

Force

Lever

Load

Pivot

46 Honey bees...
help feed the planet.

Bees transfer pollen from flower to flower as they gather nectar. This is called **pollination**.

This enables plants to reproduce by making seeds and fruit.

The work done by bees every year is worth **hundreds of billions** of dollars.

One bee colony (40,000–60,000 bees) can pollinate up to **300 million** flowers per day.

As much as **25%** of all the food we eat depends on pollination by honey bees.

Global honey bee populations have fallen rapidly in recent years. Nobody knows exactly why...

Honey bees pollinate more than **100** different food crops.

40 kinds of vegetables

50 kinds of fruits

15 kinds of nuts and seeds

Honey bees also pollinate coffee and cotton plants.

47 The deepest ocean is deeper...
than the highest mountain is high.

Sunlight Zone 0-650ft

Twilight Zone 650-3,300ft

US Navy diver
Deepest diving human
2,000ft

Midnight Zone
3,300-13,000ft

Emperor penguin
Deepest diving bird
1,850ft

Cuvier's beaked whale
Deepest diving mammal
9,500ft (1.8 miles)

Abyssal Zone
13,000-19,700ft

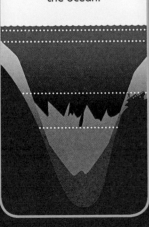

Mount Everest, the
highest mountain, is
29,029 feet above
sea level. If it was
turned upside down,
it wouldn't reach the
very bottom of
the ocean.

Hadal Zone
Below 19,700ft

Dumbo octopus
Deepest living octopus
23,000ft (4.4 miles)

Snailfish
Deepest known fish
25,000ft (4.7 miles)

Pressure at the
deepest point:
**14,200lbs
per inch²**

Challenger Deep, Pacific Ocean
Deepest place on Earth
36,069ft (6.8 miles)

48 Living in space...

is hard on human bodies.

The environment on a space station is almost weightless. Spending time living in these conditions can result in lots of serious health problems.

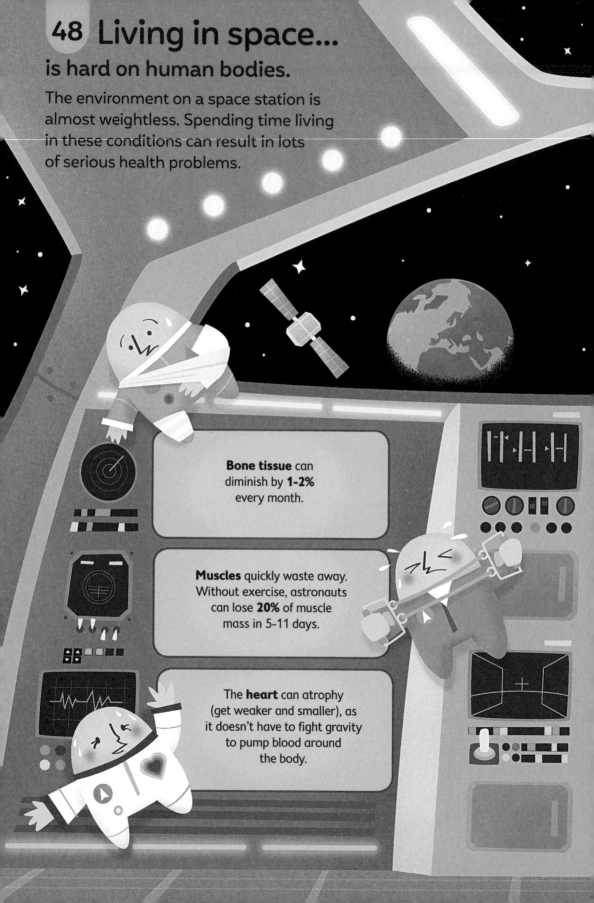

Bone tissue can diminish by **1-2%** every month.

Muscles quickly waste away. Without exercise, astronauts can lose **20%** of muscle mass in 5-11 days.

The **heart** can atrophy (get weaker and smaller), as it doesn't have to fight gravity to pump blood around the body.

In near-weightless conditions, fluids collect in astronauts' heads. The added pressure from these fluids can cause **vision problems**.

The **inner ear**, which controls balance, gets confused by weightlessness. This can cause motion sickness and vomiting.

The **spine** can stretch by **3%**, causing serious back problems.

49 50 billion cells in your body...

self-destruct every day.

A human body is made of at least
10 trillion
individual cells.

There are over **200** different types of cells in your body.
Some build body parts; others help keep your body alive.

Nucleus
Wall

Muscle, **skin** and **bone cells** make up many of your body parts.

Nerve cells pass signals from one part of the body to another.

Red blood cells carry oxygen all around your body.

White blood cells fight infections.

Some white blood cells, known as **phagocytes**, eat bacteria and clean up dead cells.

When a cell is damaged, or no longer needed, its own nucleus sends a signal to self-destruct.

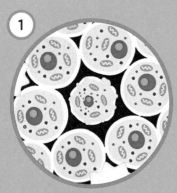

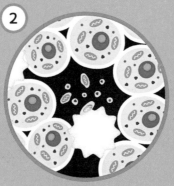

The cell shrinks, its nucleus collapses, and its wall starts to disintegrate.

The cell breaks apart completely. Phagocytes move in to clean up.

The phagocytes absorb the loose parts from the dead cell.

50 When houseflies buzz...

they always produce the musical note F.

Musical notes are caused by vibrations, such as the vibration of a guitar string – or even of a fly's wings. The rate or speed of the vibration determines how high or low the note will be.

Houseflies beat their wings about **345 times a second**.

This beating produces a particular buzzing sound – the first F above middle C.

This means you could possibly tune a guitar by listening to a buzzing fly.

51 Spider silk...

is twice as strong as steel wire.

Spider silk is a thread of protein which spiders produce to make webs.

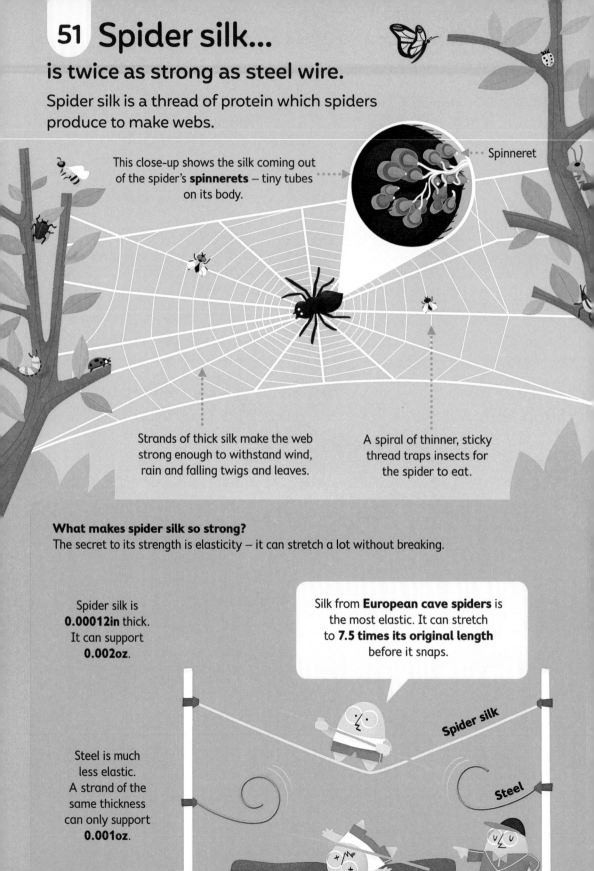

This close-up shows the silk coming out of the spider's **spinnerets** – tiny tubes on its body.

Spinneret

Strands of thick silk make the web strong enough to withstand wind, rain and falling twigs and leaves.

A spiral of thinner, sticky thread traps insects for the spider to eat.

What makes spider silk so strong?
The secret to its strength is elasticity – it can stretch a lot without breaking.

Spider silk is **0.00012in** thick. It can support **0.002oz**.

Silk from **European cave spiders** is the most elastic. It can stretch to **7.5 times its original length** before it snaps.

Spider silk

Steel is much less elastic. A strand of the same thickness can only support **0.001oz**.

Steel

52 Static electricity...

can be used to spray paint onto cars.

All materials are made of tiny **atoms** with **electrons** moving around them.

Static electricity forms when materials gain or lose electrons.

The middle of an atom has a positive charge.

Electrons have a negative charge.

If a material loses electrons it becomes positively charged.

If a material gains electrons it becomes negatively charged.

Similar charges push away from each other.

Opposite charges attract.

1 In a car factory, spray paint is connected to a machine with a positive charge. This draws electrons from the paint, leaving it with a **positive charge**.

The paint drops push away from each other, creating an even spray.

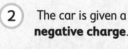

2 The car is given a **negative charge**.

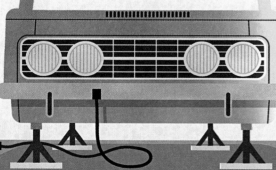

3 Opposite charges attract, so the paint is all drawn to the car. No paint splatters the floor or walls.

53 The sky isn't blue...

it's just a trick of the light.

The sky doesn't have its own color at all. When light from the Sun shines through the sky, it gets scattered around – people on the ground see the parts that get scattered the most.

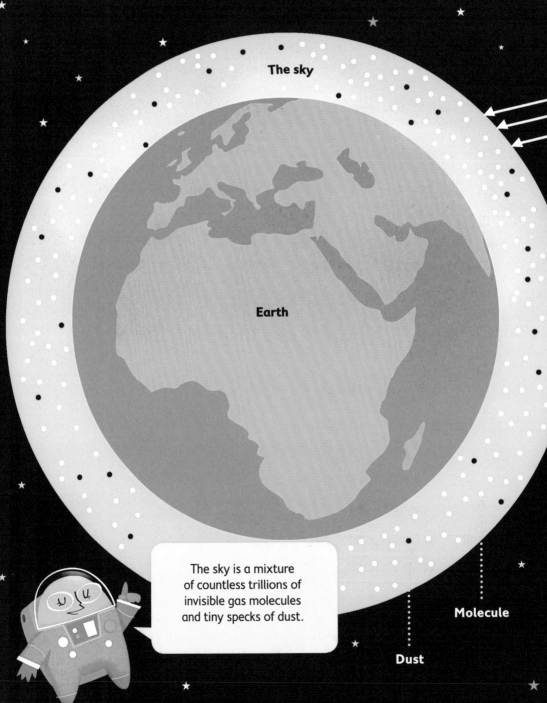

The sky

Earth

The sky is a mixture of countless trillions of invisible gas molecules and tiny specks of dust.

Molecule

Dust

Outer space is dark because there's nothing in it for light to bounce off.

The Sun

Rays of light from the Sun

Light is a form of **energy**.
White light is a mixture of all the colors of the rainbow.
Each color has a different level of energy: red has the least energy, violet has the most.

When light hits the sky...
it bumps into the gas molecules.
These scatter light all around, splitting it apart into its different colors.

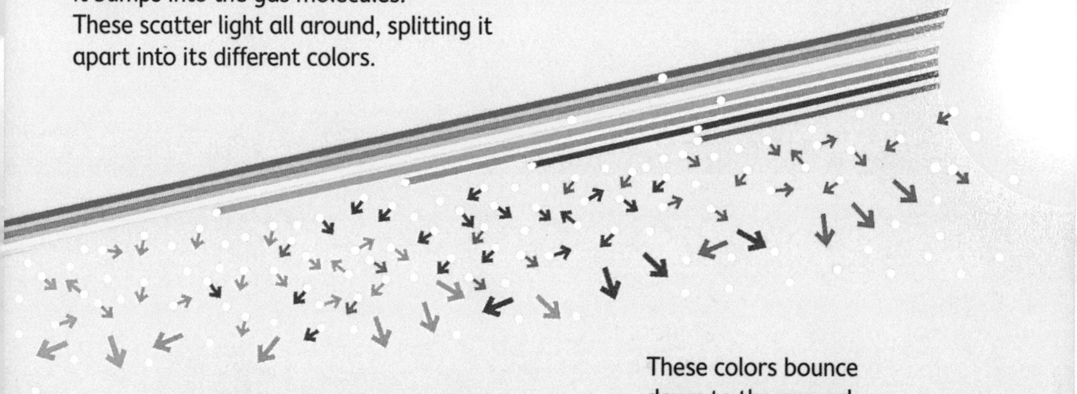

On cloudless days, violet, indigo and blue are scattered more easily than the lower energy levels of light, so they spread out the most.

These colors bounce down to the ground, creating a mix that makes the sky look pale blue.

has only one side – and only one edge.

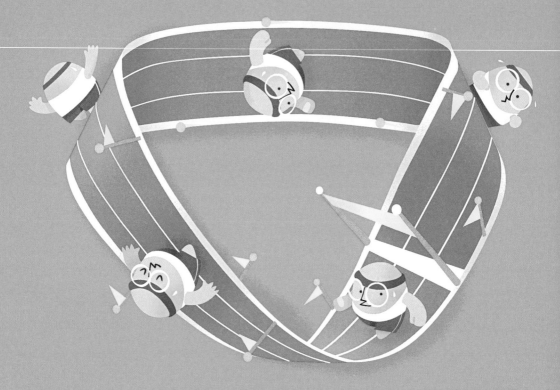

In 1858, two German mathematicians named **Möbius** and **Listing** each independently came up with the idea for this strip. Listing was the first to publish his discovery – but for some unknown reason, everyone now calls it the Möbius strip.

Try making one yourself:

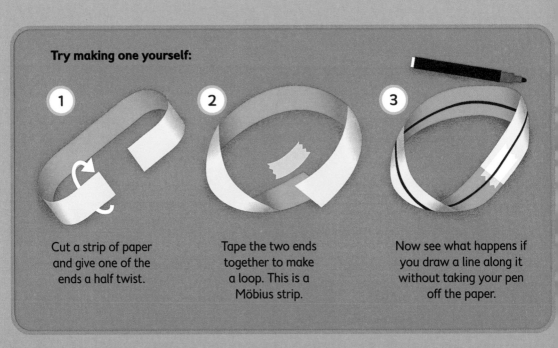

1
Cut a strip of paper and give one of the ends a half twist.

2
Tape the two ends together to make a loop. This is a Möbius strip.

3
Now see what happens if you draw a line along it without taking your pen off the paper.

55 Arctic terns migrate...

further than any other animal.

Migration is the movement of animals from one place to another.

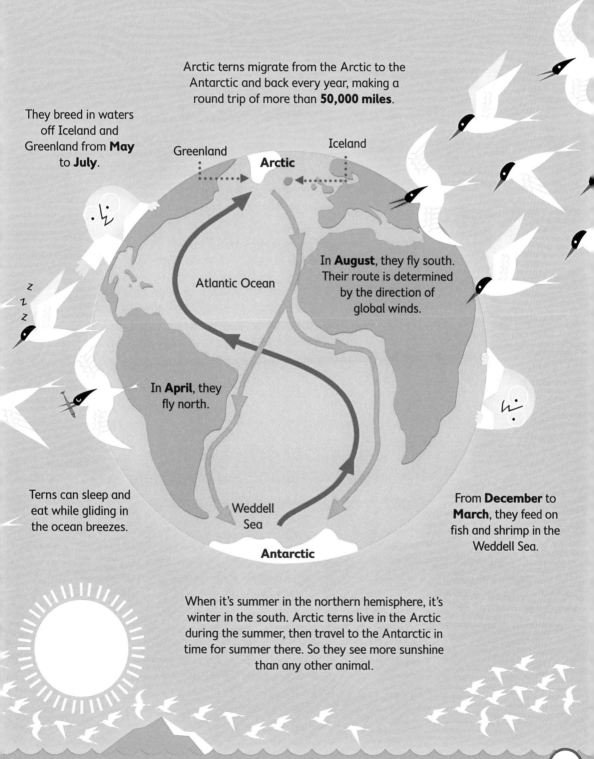

Arctic terns migrate from the Arctic to the Antarctic and back every year, making a round trip of more than **50,000 miles**.

They breed in waters off Iceland and Greenland from **May** to **July**.

Greenland

Iceland

Arctic

Atlantic Ocean

In **August**, they fly south. Their route is determined by the direction of global winds.

In **April**, they fly north.

Terns can sleep and eat while gliding in the ocean breezes.

Weddell Sea

Antarctic

From **December** to **March**, they feed on fish and shrimp in the Weddell Sea.

When it's summer in the northern hemisphere, it's winter in the south. Arctic terns live in the Arctic during the summer, then travel to the Antarctic in time for summer there. So they see more sunshine than any other animal.

Light can push...

a spaceship through the Solar System.

Light hitting an object gives it a tiny push,
called **radiation pressure**.

It's usually too small to notice – but this effect can add up.
Pressure from sunlight changes planetary orbits. It also
pushes the tails of **comets** so that they always stream away
from the Sun – no matter what direction the comet is going.

Comet

**Comet's
direction of travel**

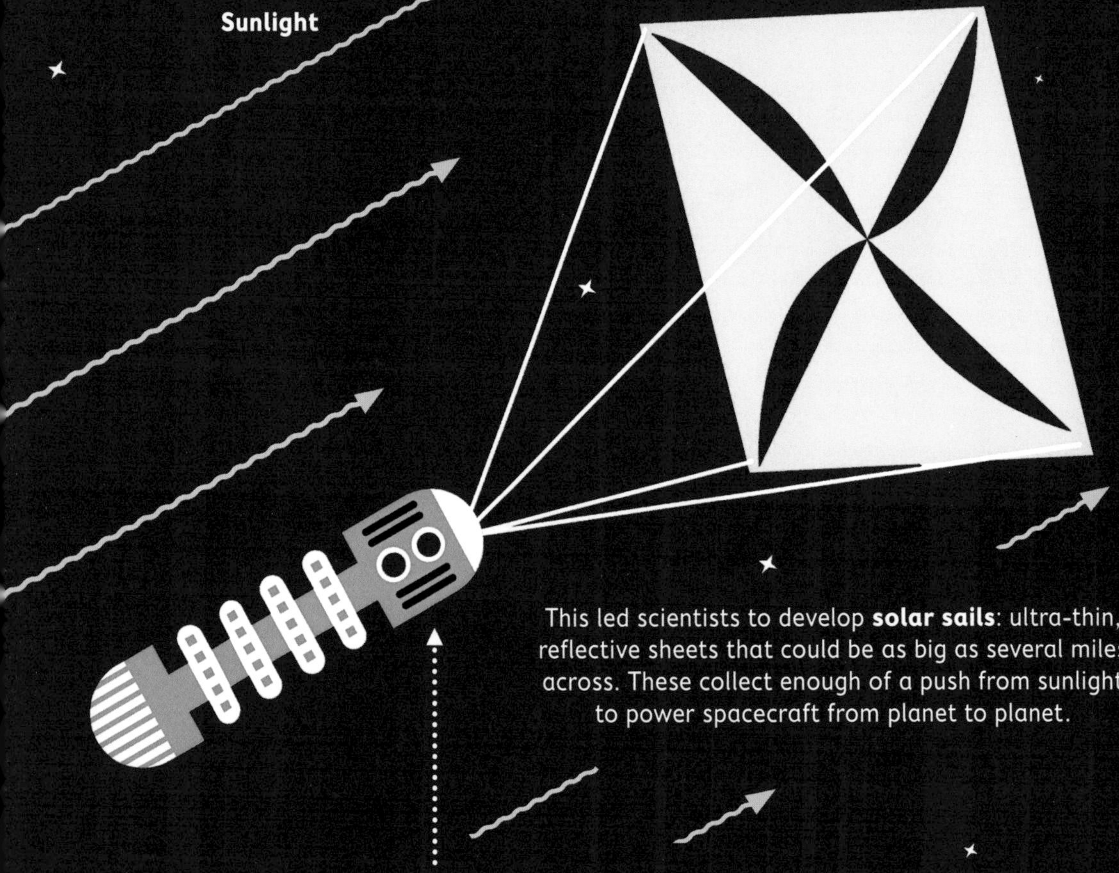

Sunlight

This led scientists to develop **solar sails**: ultra-thin,
reflective sheets that could be as big as several miles
across. These collect enough of a push from sunlight
to power spacecraft from planet to planet.

This is what **solar sail spacecraft**
of the future might look like.

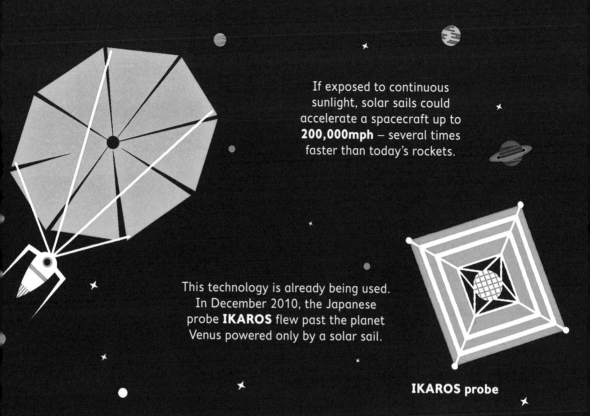

If exposed to continuous sunlight, solar sails could accelerate a spacecraft up to **200,000mph** – several times faster than today's rockets.

This technology is already being used. In December 2010, the Japanese probe **IKAROS** flew past the planet Venus powered only by a solar sail.

IKAROS probe

57 Light can squeeze...

atoms hard enough to trigger nuclear fusion.

Scientists plan to use radiation pressure to produce energy through a process known as nuclear fusion. This is how they think it will work:

1

For just a billionth of a second, a small amount of hydrogen is hit with beams of light from around **200 high-powered lasers**.

2

The lasers squeeze the hydrogen, making it **20 times denser than lead** and hotter than the Sun.

3

The **nuclei** (plural of nucleus) of two hydrogen atoms **fuse** (join together). This creates a new helium atom and releases lots of energy.

4

The energy could be collected and converted into electricity. This could provide an alternative to fossil fuels.

58 A simple lever...

can become a deadly weapon.

In the Middle Ages, the **trebuchet** was used to lob missiles at enemy castles. It was based on a simple lever.

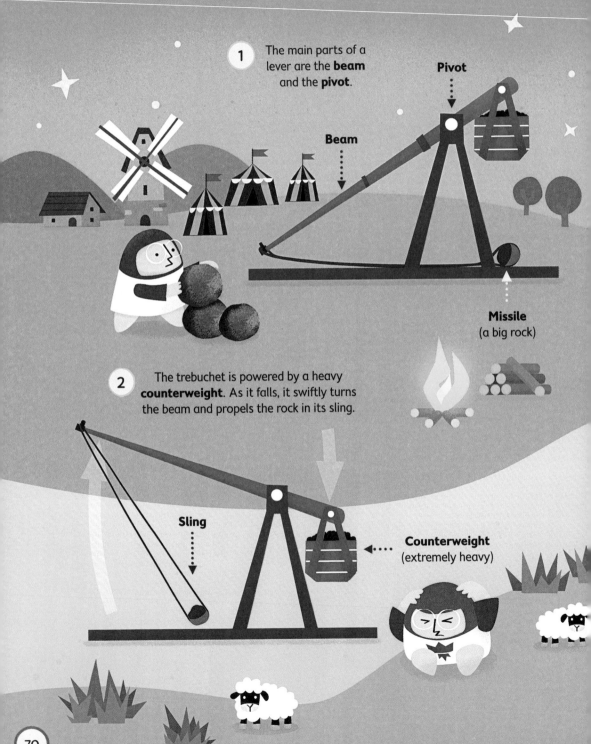

1 The main parts of a lever are the **beam** and the **pivot**.

Pivot

Beam

Missile
(a big rock)

2 The trebuchet is powered by a heavy **counterweight**. As it falls, it swiftly turns the beam and propels the rock in its sling.

Sling

Counterweight
(extremely heavy)

3 The trebuchet could launch a **330lb** stone up to **1,000ft**, crushing castle walls or enemy soldiers.

Why is the trebuchet so powerful?

Suppose it takes a trebuchet 3 seconds to launch a missile. In that time, the counterweight travels a relatively short distance **(X)**. In the same 3 seconds, the stone in the sling travels a much longer distance **(Y)**.

This means that the stone moves and gathers speed **much, much faster** than the counterweight, which gives it a lot of force when it leaves the sling.

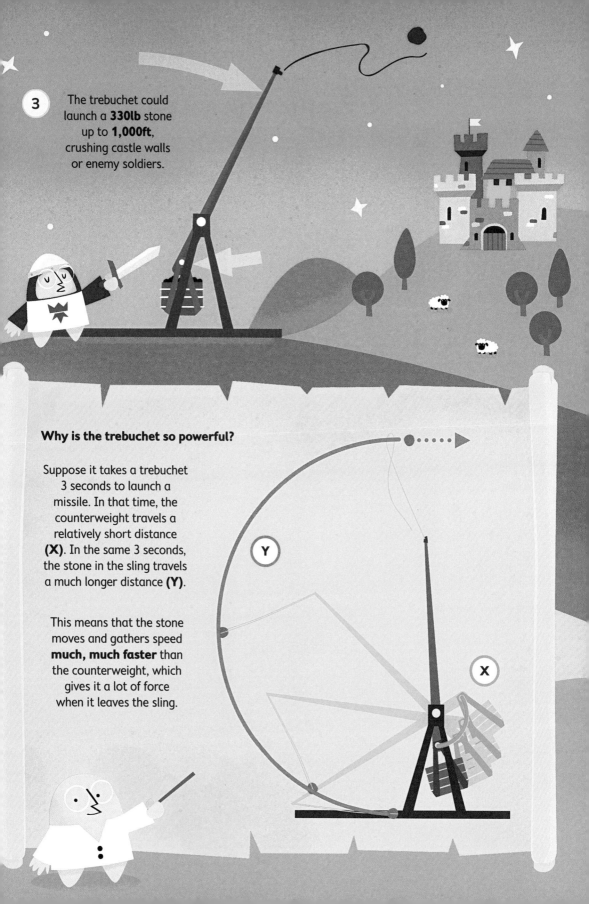

59 Days on Earth...

are getting longer and longer.

The pull of the Moon's gravity is slowing down the Earth's rotation.
Every million years, our days get **20 seconds** longer.

	Hours per day	Days per year
620 million years ago	21.9	400
230 million years ago	22.7	386
Present day	24	365
180 million years from now	25	350

60 Six feet of DNA...

can fit in a cell too small to see.

DNA is a chain of molecules found in living cells that contains coded instructions for building and running an organism.

A typical human cell is about **0.0004 inches** across, and can't be seen with the naked eye. However, if all the DNA in a cell were unraveled, it would be about **6 feet** long.

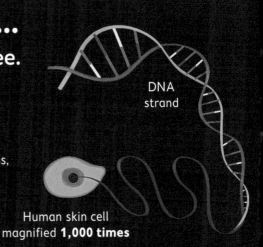

DNA strand

Human skin cell magnified **1,000 times**

Stretched end to end, all the DNA in one human body would reach to the Sun and back more than **250 times**.

61 Some seeds...

can travel thousands of miles.

By exploding

Some seeds grow in pods. When the pods dry, they can suddenly burst open and shoot their seeds into the air.

Wisteria

By flying

Light and feathery dandelion seeds can sail on the breeze.

Impatiens

By spreading their seeds over a wide area, plants make it more likely that some of their offspring will survive.

Maples have winged seeds (called samaras) that spin, flutter and drift in the wind.

By hitch-hiking

When birds eat berries, the seeds in the fruit come out later in the bird's droppings — many miles away.

By floating

Coconut trees have seeds that float. They can ride ocean currents over distances of **1,000 miles** or more.

Burdock seeds have dozens of tiny hooks that catch on to passing animals.

62 Charles Darwin...

changed the way we think about life on Earth.

Darwin was an English naturalist who came up with a theory to explain how all species evolve, or change, over time. It made him famous, but it also upset some people because it went against their religious beliefs.

1809
Charles Darwin was born in Shropshire, England.

1828-1831
Darwin studied at Cambridge University.

1831
He set sail on HMS *Beagle*. Over the next five years, he studied thousands of animals around the world.

1859
He finally published it in *On the Origin of Species by Means of Natural Selection or the Preservation of Favoured Races in the Struggle for Life*.

1839-1859
Darwin spent over 20 years developing his theory of evolution.

1860
Some religious leaders attacked Darwin's theory. He and his supporters defended it, pointing to the evidence he had collected.

1882
Darwin died at age 73.

63 Evolution...

is happening all the time.

Darwin argued that living things evolve because of a process he called **natural selection**. This is how he came up with his theory.

Darwin's observations

1 Darwin saw that food in the wild is limited, and that living things have to fight for it.

Living things compete with each other to survive.

2 He studied thousands of different individual plants and animals, including lots and lots of...

Barnacles   Orchids   Ducks

Every individual living thing is unique.

3 He bred pigeons to prove something most people already suspected.

Mother   Father

Stripes inherited   Color inherited
from father   from mother

Features are passed on from parents to their offspring.

Darwin's conclusions

All individuals are competing for food...

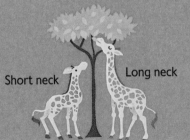

Short neck   Long neck

The feature becomes more common with each generation that goes by...

...so the ones that have a feature that gives them an advantage, such as a long neck for reaching leaves, will be more likely to survive.

They will then reproduce and pass on that feature to their offspring.

...and eventually the whole species has it. This process is happening all the time in every species of living thing.

Darwin called this process **natural selection**.

EVOLUTION

64 During hibernation...

some animals stop breathing completely.

Hibernation is a state that allows animals to survive the cold winter months when there is little food. Here's how it works:

Dormice prepare for hibernation by eating nuts – a good source of energy.

Dormice hibernate in nests of leaves. Their temperature and heartbeat drop, so they use little energy. This lets them survive seven months without eating.

Body temperature falls from 90°F to 45°F.

Heartbeat drops from 500 to 10 beats per minute.

Breathing falls to 2-3 times per minute.

Woodfrogs hibernate under leaves or a shallow layer of soil.

When the weather gets warmer, their bodies defrost and they start breathing again.

1

2

3

As the weather gets colder, ice crystals form in their blood and they stop breathing.

Doctors can use a form of hibernation to treat patients with serious wounds.

The patient's blood is replaced with chilled salt water to cool the body rapidly.

At 50°F, the patient stops breathing, the body slows and stops needing oxygen from blood. This allows doctors to operate without risk of brain damage. Blood is then pumped back in to revive the patient.

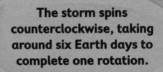

65 Jupiter's Great Red Spot...

is a violent storm that's bigger than Earth.

The Great Red Spot is by far the largest storm in the Solar System. It has been raging for over 400 years.

Jupiter is
1,300
times bigger
than Earth.

The Great Red Spot is approximately
10,000
miles wide.

Earth is shown here in scale to Jupiter.

The Great Red Spot

Winds inside the storm reach
250mph.

Within the storm, there are lightning bolts thousands of times brighter than those on Earth.

The storm spins counterclockwise, taking around six Earth days to complete one rotation.

66 Whales have finger bones...

even though they don't have fingers.

Whales and humans are both **mammals**, and they share a common ancestor. That ancestor passed on a similar bone structure to all its descendants.

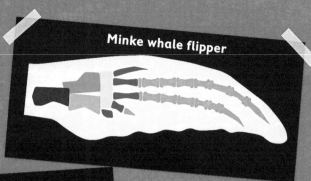

Minke whale flipper

Human arm

So, although whales have evolved separately for **hundreds of millions of years**, there are still remarkable similarities between whale flippers and human arms.

Bones shared by humans and whales:	**Phalanges** (finger bones)	**Radius**
	Metacarpals (hand bones)	**Ulna**
	Carpals (wrist bones)	**Humerus**

A similar basic bone structure can also be found in other mammals:

Cat Bat Horse

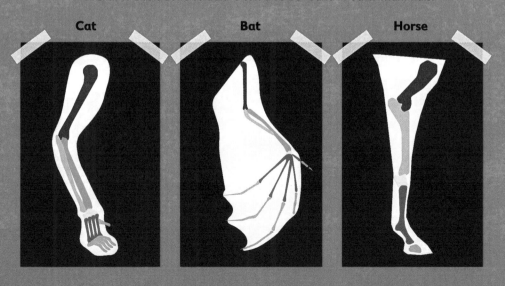

67 Whales once walked...

on all fours.

Whales are descended from **four-legged animals** that lived on land. They evolved over time, adapting more and more to life in the sea.

52 million years ago:
One early ancestor, **Pakicetus**, lived on land but hunted fish in shallow water.

50 million years ago:
Its descendant **Ambulocetus** lived in and out of the water, like a sea lion.

45 million years ago:
Rodhocetus was clumsy on land, but a strong, flexible tail made it a great swimmer.

40 million years ago:
Dorudon was fully aquatic, but this ancestor of the whale still had tiny hind legs.

Today:
The **Humpback whale** spends its entire life in the water and has no hind legs.

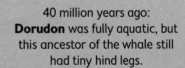

68 Science fiction stories...

have inspired many real inventions.

First published in 1870
TWENTY THOUSAND LEAGUES UNDER THE SEA
BY JULES VERNE

Science fiction
A professor and his crew are rescued by the mysterious Nemo, captain of the *Nautilus*, a ship that can travel under water.

Real invention
Engineer Simon Lake was determined to make Verne's fictional ship a reality. In 1896, he built the first metal **submarine with an airlock** to let people in and out under water.

"With its untold depths, couldn't the sea keep alive specimens of life from another age?"

First published in 1942
WALDO: GENIUS IN ORBIT
BY ROBERT HEINLEIN

Science fiction
Irritable genius Waldo F. Jones, a recluse living in space, builds mechanical arms to help him cope with a muscle-weakening disease.

Real invention
In 1945, a team at NASA built their own **robot arms**, and named them 'waldoes'. These arms are used today to help repair spacecraft.

"Waldo pursed his lips. 'The welfare of nameless Earth crawlers is not my concern!'"

First published in 1897

WAR OF THE WORLDS
BY H. G. WELLS

Science fiction
Invaders from the planet Mars travel to Earth and attack using giant machines called tripods.

Real invention
Physicist Robert Goddard was so entranced by the idea of interplanetary travel that he spent his life designing **space rockets**. His earliest models took off in 1926.

"Across the gulf of space, intellects vast and cool regarded this earth with envious eyes."

First published in 1961

DIAL 'F'
FOR FRANKENSTEIN
BY ARTHUR C. CLARKE

Science fiction
Telephones in people's homes all across the globe begin to talk to each other in a network, creating an artificial mind that causes chaos.

Real invention
Computer scientist Tim Berners-Lee was inspired by the idea of the network. In 1990, he activated the **World Wide Web**, which connects computers across telephone lines.

"At 01:50 GMT on December 1, 1975, every telephone in the world started to ring."

A space elevator...

could lift future astronauts into orbit.

Scientists are working on a plan to stretch a giant cable from the Earth's surface straight up into outer space. Passenger vehicles would climb up and down the cable – without burning loads of fuel.

Counterweight
A large mass that keeps the cable tightly stretched. Possibly a captured asteroid.

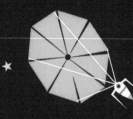

Space station
Interplanetary space flights could dock here.

A space elevator could be safer and more environmentally friendly than rockets.

Once built, it would make getting to space much cheaper.

Today's rocket flights each cost

100 times

the estimated cost of an elevator ride into orbit.

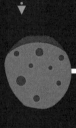

Elevator cars
Also called 'climbers'. A
voyage up or down could
take as long as a week.

The cars could be powered
by electricity, sunlight, or
even lasers.

Cable
Made of super-strong and
light material.

The entire cable would
be about **62,000 miles**
long. That's long enough
to wrap around the Earth
2.5 times.

Anchor station
A floating platform
located on the Equator.

Some scientists believe
that a space elevator
could be built in just
50 years' time.

70 Octopuses...

have three hearts.

Two of their hearts pump blood through their **gills** (organs that enable them to breathe under water) and one pumps blood through the rest of their bodies.

Octopus eyes have slit-shaped **pupils**. No matter which way the octopus turns, the slit remains horizontal.

Octopuses don't have any **bones** in their bodies, and can squeeze through very tiny spaces.

Double rows of **suction cups** on their arms can be used to grip things – and can taste whatever they touch.

Octopus **ink** can blind a predator and block its sense of smell, while masking the octopus's escape.

Octopus arms can act independently. Two-thirds of an octopus's **neurons** (nerve cells that transmit information) are located in its arms.

Before speedy modern calculators and electronic computers were invented, teams of people known as **computers** did complex calculations by hand.

In 1757, three French scientists spent **five months on a single calculation**. They wanted to predict the exact course of Halley's Comet around the Sun.

They made their prediction by splitting the calculation into a series of much smaller parts.

In the late 19th century, a group of women at Harvard University known as the **Harvard Computers** cataloged and classified thousands of stars by hand.

They received little credit or pay – but they made important discoveries. Several of the women, such as **Henrietta Swan Leavitt**, later became famous astronomers.

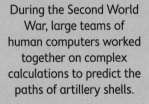

During the Second World War, large teams of human computers worked together on complex calculations to predict the paths of artillery shells.

Soldiers on the battlefield relied on their results to adjust their aim.

use echoes to catch their prey.

Bats hunt at night, but many types of bat can't see in the dark. Instead, they use a technique called **echolocation**.

1 Bats can make high-pitched noises, called **ultrasounds**.

Ultrasounds are so high-pitched that humans can't hear them.

2 Ultrasounds bounce back off solid things. Bats pinpoint their prey by listening to the echoes.

3 By sending out a series of ultrasounds, bats can tell if there is something moving in the darkness.

4 Some insects, such as tiger moths, send out ultrasounds of their own. This prevents bats from detecting them.

73 Limestone caves...
are carved out of rock by water.

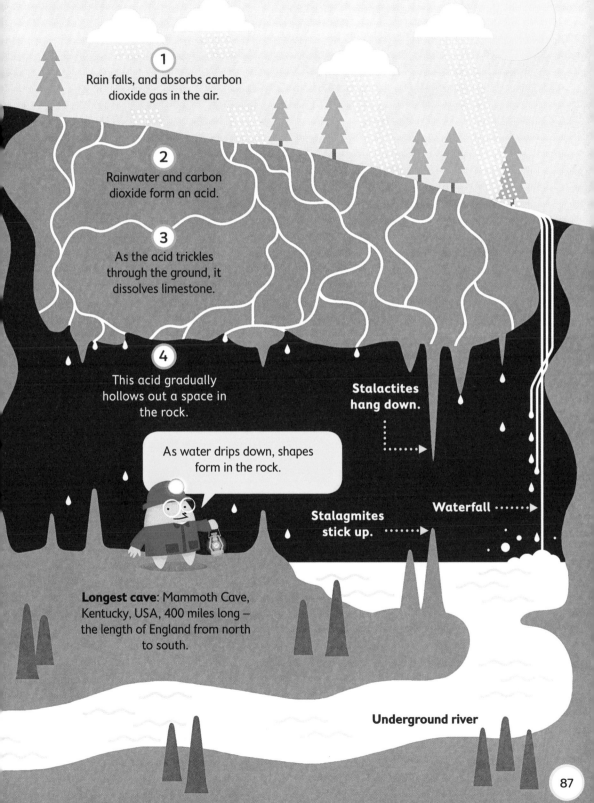

1 Rain falls, and absorbs carbon dioxide gas in the air.

2 Rainwater and carbon dioxide form an acid.

3 As the acid trickles through the ground, it dissolves limestone.

4 This acid gradually hollows out a space in the rock.

As water drips down, shapes form in the rock.

Stalactites hang down. · · · · · · · ·▶

Stalagmites stick up. · · · · · · · ·▶

Waterfall · · · · · · · ·▶

Longest cave: Mammoth Cave, Kentucky, USA, 400 miles long – the length of England from north to south.

Underground river

Jupiter...

has at least 79 moons.

A moon is a lump of rock that goes around a planet, in the same way as planets go around the Sun.

How many moons does each planet in the Solar System have?

Mercury	Venus	Earth	Mars
0	0	1	2

Jupiter	Saturn	Uranus	Neptune
79	82	27	14

Jupiter's moons

Jupiter is an enormous planet. This gives it a very strong gravitational pull that holds lots of moons in orbit around it. Here are three of its most interesting moons:

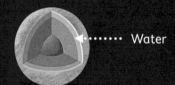

·········· Water

Europa
(with a section cut away)

Io

Scientists think there is water beneath the surface of **Europa**. This means it may be able to support life.

Io has over 400 active volcanoes – more than any other place in the Solar System.

Ganymede is the largest moon in the Solar System. It's bigger than the planet Mercury.

Ganymede

Mercury

75 Around 4,000 earthquakes...

happen every single day.

The size of an earthquake is measured on a scale called the **Moment Magnitude Scale**.

10	Devastation, many deaths
9	
8	Buildings collapse, landslides
7	
6	Cracks in buildings, falling branches
5	Windows rattle or break, light damage
4	
3	Vibrations detected
2	Barely noticeable
1	

Earthquakes in an average year:

1 earthquake size 8 or higher

145,000 earthquakes size 3.1-7.9

1,300,000 earthquakes size 3 or lower

The energy released at each level is **32** times greater than the previous level.

An earthquake in Sumatra, Indonesia, in 2004 measured **9.3** on the Moment Magnitude Scale and caused more than **200,000** deaths.

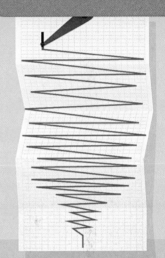

How an earthquake happens

1. The Earth's crust is made up of rocky plates which are slowly moving.

2. When plates rub against each other, pressure builds on rocks in the ground.

3. Rocks suddenly crack and slide past each other, releasing energy and making the ground shake.

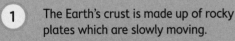

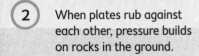

Epicenter ····▸ •

Rock here moves up.

This is the **focus**, where the earthquake starts. The point on the ground above the focus is called the epicenter.

Rock here moves down.

◂····· This is where the rock breaks.

76 Remembering a memory...

creates a new memory.

You create memories all the time, based on information from your senses. But because of the way your brain works, it's impossible to *remember* those memories without altering them, creating a *new* memory.

You think with the front part of your brain – the **conscious region**.

Creating a memory

When you experience something, cells in your brain pass on information to each other. This forms a unique route through your brain, called an **information pathway**. This creates a new memory in the conscious region of your brain.

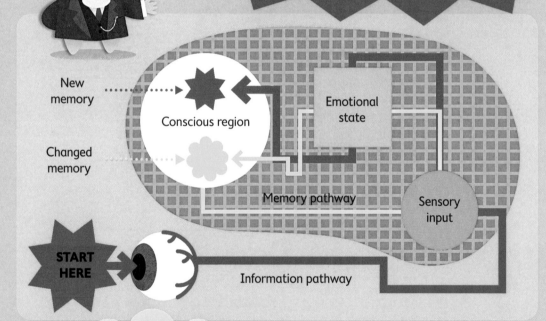

New memory

Conscious region

Changed memory

Emotional state

Memory pathway

Sensory input

START HERE

Information pathway

Remembering a memory

To recall the experience, your conscious region creates a **memory pathway**. This tries to retrace the *original* information pathway. But the pathway starts from a different place...

...and can easily get mixed up by different emotions. So your brain ends up creating a *new*, subtly changed memory.

77 Your nose can detect...

up to a trillion different smells.

We take more than **20,000 breaths** per day. Each one is packed with scents and aromas that give us essential information about our surroundings.

Our sense of smell warns us of dangers, such as fire or gas, tells us what foods are safest to eat, and can even help predict the weather.

Every person has his or her own smell. This smell, based on things such as genetics and diet, is *as unique as a fingerprint.*

Many parents can identify their children by smell.

The way food *tastes* depends mostly on its *smell.* That's why nothing tastes as good when you have a stuffy nose.

78 Albert Einstein was so clever...

a doctor stole his brain after he died.

At age 26, Einstein was a lawyer's clerk who studied physics in his spare time. He managed to explain the link between time and space, and paved the way for a new branch of physics, called **quantum mechanics**.

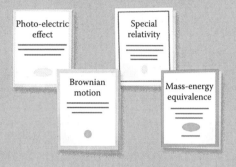

Photo-electric effect

Special relativity

Brownian motion

Mass-energy equivalence

1879
Albert Einstein was born in Ulm, Germany, to a Jewish family.

1884
At age 5, Albert was fascinated by the unseen force that made the needle on a compass move.

1905
Einstein published four separate physics papers in one year. Each explained a fundamental principle of the Universe.

1933
He escaped from the Nazi regime in Germany to England, and then emigrated to the USA.

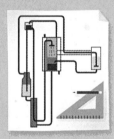

1926
Together with his student Leo Szilard, Einstein designed a new type of refrigerator.

1921
Einstein won a Nobel Prize for his paper explaining the photo-electric effect.

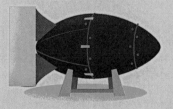

1940
Einstein persuaded the US President to build an atom bomb before the Nazis managed to build their own.

1955
Einstein died at age 76.

Against his wishes, part of Einstein's brain was preserved. Scientists are still studying it to see if they can find out what made him a genius.

79 Einstein changed the world...

with his discovery: $E = mc^2$.

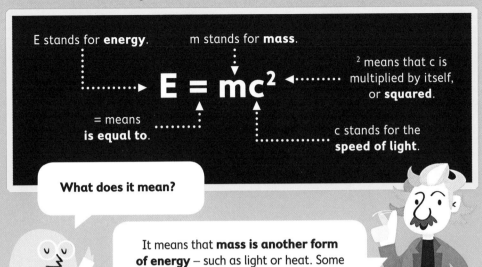

E stands for **energy**.

m stands for **mass**.

$$E = mc^2$$

= means **is equal to**.

² means that c is multiplied by itself, or **squared**.

c stands for the **speed of light**.

What does it mean?

It means that **mass is another form of energy** – such as light or heat. Some earlier scientists thought this was the case, but no one could prove it.

Building on Einstein's discovery, scientists in Europe developed machines that could smash atoms together and convert some of their mass into heat.

1 Inside an atom-smasher, a single particle from one atom hurtles into another atom's nucleus.

2 That nucleus splits apart, and releases lots and lots of heat.

Engineers found world-changing ways to harness this release of energy, known as **nuclear fission**.

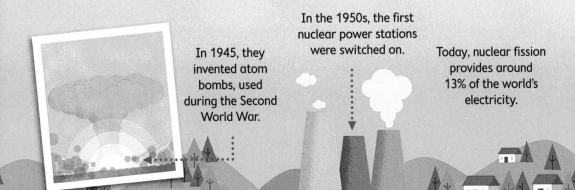

In 1945, they invented atom bombs, used during the Second World War.

In the 1950s, the first nuclear power stations were switched on.

Today, nuclear fission provides around 13% of the world's electricity.

80 Pure luck...
can lead to big discoveries.

In 1945, American engineer Percy Spencer was working on radar technology that used **microwaves** to detect enemy ships and planes.

One day, Spencer noticed that the high-powered microwaves were melting a chocolate bar in his pocket.

He then tried using microwaves to cook popcorn – and so discovered the technology for the **microwave oven**.

Here are some other examples.

In 1964, astronomers Arno Penzias and Robert Wilson accidentally detected some low-level radiation in outer space. It turned out to be key evidence supporting the **Big Bang Theory**.

Chance favors only the prepared mind.

PASTEUR

In 1928, Alexander Fleming found mold growing on an old experiment. He had discovered a form of **penicillin**, a medicine that has since saved millions of lives.

PENICILLIN

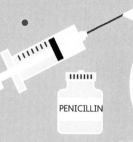

In 1835, Francis Pettit Smith designed a **screw propeller**. During testing, it broke in half – and to Smith's surprise the boat started moving much faster. He promptly changed his design to make the propeller half as long.

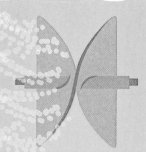

French scientist Louis Pasteur made several accidental discoveries. He pointed out that it takes a good scientist to recognize the importance of a stroke of luck.

81 Butterflies and bees...

drink crocodile tears.

Some insects make a habit of sipping other animals' tears. This tear-feeding is called **lachryphagy**.

Why do they do it? Tears are full of nutrients and minerals that may not be part of an insect's normal diet of nectar and pollen.

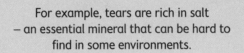

For example, tears are rich in salt – an essential mineral that can be hard to find in some environments.

Crocodiles cry whenever they eat. Scientists don't really understand why.

82 Insects outnumber humans...

by about 200 million to one.

How many insects are there? Scientists estimate that the total number is around **1.4 quintillion**. That's **1,400,000,000,000,000,000** insects.

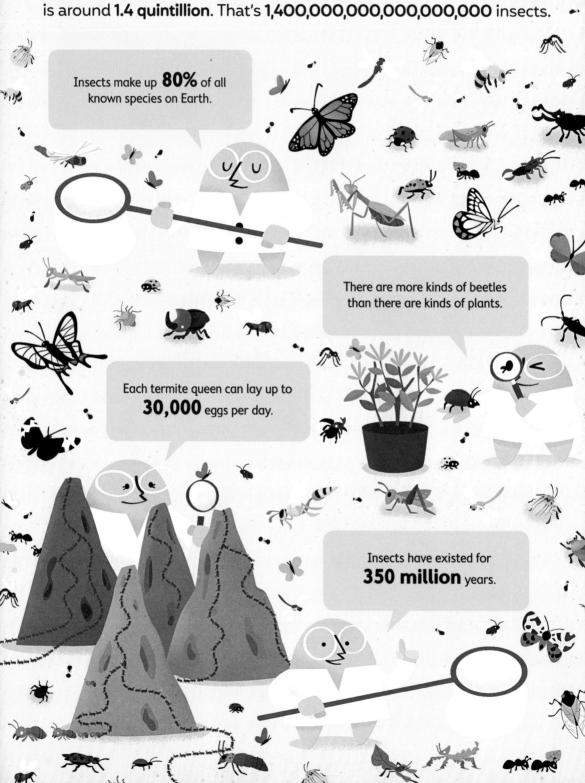

Insects make up **80%** of all known species on Earth.

There are more kinds of beetles than there are kinds of plants.

Each termite queen can lay up to **30,000** eggs per day.

Insects have existed for **350 million** years.

83 Iron...

makes up 95% of all metal we use.

Iron comes from rock in the ground called iron ore.

Iron ore

Iron ore mine
Holes are drilled in the rock and filled with explosives to blast out the iron ore.

The ore is taken to a crusher.

Crusher
The crusher breaks the ore into small chunks.

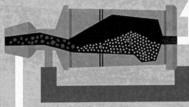

Iron ore powder | Waste

Grinder
The chunks are ground into powder.

Processor
Magnets separate iron ore powder, which is magnetic, from any waste material.

Pellet maker
Iron ore powder is turned into pellets.

Train
Most of the iron is taken by train to a steel factory.

Steel factory
Iron is made into steel, a mixture of iron and carbon, which is harder and stronger than iron.

Blast furnace
The pellets are heated with carbon and limestone. This removes oxygen from the iron ore leaving pure iron.

Steel is used to make many things, from silverware and washing machines, to bridges and skyscrapers.

84 Pencils and diamonds...

are made of the same thing.

They're made of carbon, which can form completely different substances, depending on how the atoms are arranged.

Diamond
Each carbon atom is bonded to four others. This makes its structure extremely strong.

Diamond is one of the hardest materials on Earth. It is used for industrial drilling.

Graphite
Carbon atoms are arranged in layers. These slide over each other easily.

Graphite is used in pencils. Layers of atoms slip off the pencil and onto paper, leaving a black mark.

Graphene
A single layer of graphite. It is amazingly thin — only one atom thick. It is very strong, flexible and light.

Graphene is a new material. It was developed in a lab in 2004.

Scientists think it will be used to make lots of things in the future, such as bendable screens for phones.

65 It may be raining diamonds...
on Jupiter.

Jupiter is a **gas giant**: a planet made mostly of gas, possibly with a rocky core. Temperatures and pressures inside Jupiter's atmosphere are so high that it *could* produce a rain of **liquid diamonds**.

1
Lightning storms ignite **methane gas** in the planet's upper atmosphere.

2
This produces **carbon soot**, which forms into clumps of **graphite**.

3
As they fall toward the planet's core, the clumps are compressed, forming **diamonds**.

4
At temperatures over **14,400°F (8,000°C)**, the diamonds melt and fall like raindrops.

Jupiter's core

86 A Victorian scientist...

designed a mechanical, steam-powered computer.

The first-ever programmable computer, called the **Analytical Engine**, was designed by English scientist Charles Babbage in the 19th century. Sadly, it was never completed.

The plans for the Analytical Engine called for tens of thousands of metal cogs, wheels, nuts and bolts, combining to make a machine over **13 feet tall** and **20 feet long**.

The Engine would have been able to solve complex mathematical equations. Like modern computers, it had separate **processing** and **memory** units, and ways of entering **data** and printing results.

This illustration shows part of the plan of the Analytical Engine, as seen from above.

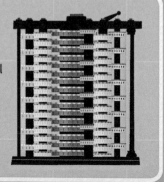

Seen from the side, the Analytical Engine might have looked something like this.

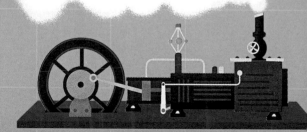

A **steam engine** would have been used to turn the machine's heavy columns of interlocking gears and wheels.

87 The first computer coder...

was an English countess.

Augusta Ada King, Countess of Lovelace, was a talented amateur scientist. She quickly grasped the potential of the Analytical Engine.

The Engine was meant to be **coded**, or **programmed**, using cards with holes punched through them. In 1843, Ada published a sample program for these cards.

Had the Engine been completed, Ada's program would have enabled it to calculate a famously complex series of numbers known as the **Bernoulli numbers**.

This is widely considered to be the first ever computer program.

88 Narwhals...

are helping oceanographers.

Narwhals fitted with temperature sensors have provided scientists with new data from the Arctic depths.

Oceanographers study the oceans. They have long been tracking the oceans' rising temperature...

...but, in the winter, taking measurements below the thick Arctic ice is difficult and expensive. So, in 2006 and 2007, a team of scientists came up with a plan.

1. They attached sensors to **14 narwhals**. The narwhals swam far under the ice, and their sensors beamed up depth and temperature data.

Sensor

2. The data showed that the Arctic is warming even more quickly than expected.

3. After six or seven months, the sensors fell off, leaving the narwhals unharmed.

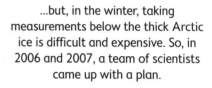

Narwhals regularly dive to depths of **5,600ft (over a mile)** beneath the surface.

Male narwhals have a very long tooth, or **tusk**. They use it to impress females and rival males.

89 The Sun...

makes up 99.8% of all the matter in the Solar System.

The Sun is the star at the center of the Solar System. It is a gigantic ball of burning matter, which sends heat and light millions of miles into space.

The Sun is **900,000 miles** wide.
Over 1.3 million Earths would fit inside it.

Elements that make up the Sun:

74% Hydrogen

25% Helium

1% Other

Unmanned spacecraft orbit the Sun. It's so hot that the closest they can get is about **25 million miles** from the surface.

Heat shield ····▶

Solar panels provide power.

Instruments collect information and send back pictures.

Earth is **93 million miles** away from the Sun.

On the surface, the Sun is at least **10,000°F (5,500°C)**.

The heat comes from the core, where the temperature can reach **27 million°F (15 million°C)**.

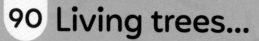

90 Living trees...

are mostly dead.

Up to **99%** of a tree is made up of dead cells. Only the leaves, buds, root tips, and a thin layer of cells beneath the bark are actually alive.

Beneath a tree's bark is a layer of living tissue just one or two cells thick. It is called the **cambium**, and it is essential to a tree's survival.

On its outer side, the cambium makes **phloem** – a living tissue that carries food from the leaves to the roots.

On its inner side, it makes **xylem** – a dead tissue that carries water from the roots to the leaves.

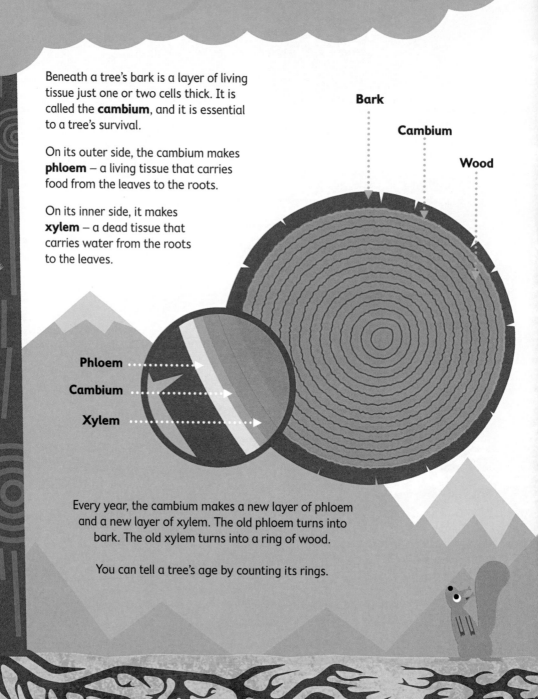

Bark

Cambium

Wood

Phloem

Cambium

Xylem

Every year, the cambium makes a new layer of phloem and a new layer of xylem. The old phloem turns into bark. The old xylem turns into a ring of wood.

You can tell a tree's age by counting its rings.

91 Pen-tailed tree shrews...

drink alcohol every evening.

Pen-tailed tree shrews from Malaysia spend two hours
a night sipping the sugary juice or nectar of Bertam palms.

The woody flower of the palm produces
nectar that ferments with natural yeast to
form a juice with a high alcohol content of up
to 3.8% – the same as many beers.

As the tree shrew
scampers from flower
to flower, it helps
pollinate the palm.

This tree shrew is the size of a
small rat. Its tiny body is able to
break down the alcohol quickly.

92 Rocks from space...
land on Earth all the time.

Small rocks in space are called **meteoroids**. Meteoroid maximum width: 13ft

Rocks in space are called **asteroids**. Asteroid average width: 130ft

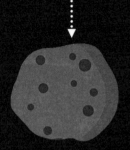

Asteroids and meteoroids burn up when they fall through the sky. These flaming rocks are called **meteors**.

Big chunks that land on Earth are called **meteorites**.

Every day, enough meteor dust falls on Earth to fill up a school bus.

93 Planet Earth...
is constantly losing weight.

As much as **100,000 tons** of gas in Earth's atmosphere disappears into space every year – the same as the weight of an aircraft carrier.

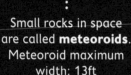

Earth's atmosphere is a mixture of different gases.

The two lightest gases – hydrogen and helium – gradually float to the top of the atmosphere...

When a helium balloon deflates, the helium gas inside it eventually reaches outer space.

He

H

H

He

H

He

He

...and escape into outer space.

Hydrogen

H

He

H

H

H

The weight lost each year amounts to a fraction of 1% of the planet's total weight.

Helium

He

He

He

H

Many inventions...

were inspired by the natural world.

A sticky secret

A Swiss inventor named George de Mestral was fed up with his dog getting covered in sticker burrs.

Mestral copied the idea to create **Velcro**® – a fabric made in two halves. One is covered in hooks that sticks to another, covered in tiny loops.

A close-up examination of the burrs revealed the secret of their stickiness – hundreds of tiny hooks.

Solar power

Plants convert sunlight to energy that they can use to grow, through a process called **photosynthesis**.

Solar panels convert sunlight to electricity using man-made materials called **semiconductors**.

Inventors are developing solar panels that produce electricity by combining semiconductors with **bacteria** that can photosynthesize.

Energy conversion rate: **3-6%**

Energy conversion rate: **20%**

Expected energy conversion rate: **30%**

Water catcher

Beetles in the Namib Desert have very bumpy shells that collect dew from morning fog.

A team of engineers in the US has created small plastic domes that mimic the beetles' bumps.

These domes are used as portable dew collectors, to help people in dry places gather drinking water.

95 Random numbers...

aren't always random.

Random numbers are used in everything from secret codes to the lottery – but truly random numbers are very difficult to create.

A series of truly random numbers isn't based on any recognizable pattern.

Rolling dice is a good way to generate random numbers, but it is very slow.

Computers can create lots of random numbers very quickly.

But they can only follow specific instructions, and so behave very predictably. By making *random numbers* in a *non-random way*, computers produce numbers that *aren't* perfectly random.

Keeping secrets

The codes that keep emails and online information private are based on series of random numbers.

The less random those numbers are, the easier it is for **hackers** to crack the codes.

The quickest way to create truly random numbers is to feed computers data from events in nature that are completely chaotic and *unpredictable*. Scientists have done this by...

...counting particles as they ping off radioactive substances.

...measuring variations in radio static caused by thunderstorms.

...taking readings of the changing patterns in lava lamps.

96 The blackest black...

is helping scientists see deeper into space.

All visible materials, whatever color they are, reflect some light. But scientists have created a material so black that it reflects just **0.04%** of the light that hits it. Objects coated in this don't appear to have any texture. They resemble empty space or a black hole.

The material is made by arranging **carbon nanotubes** (hollow, microscopic strands of carbon) on a metal sheet.

Each nanotube is **10,000 times thinner** than a human hair.

A ray of light

The nanotubes form a kind of dense carpet, where light gets trapped and absorbed instead of bouncing off.

Astronomers will use this material to line the insides of **space telescopes**. This will stop extra light from scattering onto sensitive light detectors, resulting in clearer pictures of distant objects.

Similar surfaces also exist in nature. **Gaboon pit vipers** have micro-ridges on their scales that absorb light – enabling them to blend into their environment.

97 The noisiest reefs...

are the healthiest reefs.

Roughly **a quarter** of all marine species live in coral reefs. Scientists have found that noisier reefs have more living creatures, healthier coral, and are better at attracting new residents.

Many species of fish make **grunting**, **thumping** or **croaking** sounds.

Shrimp make **popping** and **snapping** sounds with their claws.

Reef noises can carry for several miles under water.

Baby fish, shrimp and crabs swimming in the open ocean can recognize the sound of a healthy reef – and it may help them to choose their future home.

Sea urchin spines **crackle** as they tap against each other.

Feeding parrotfish **crunch** and **grind** mouthfuls of hard coral.

Coral reefs are under serious threat from climate change and overfishing. By listening to reefs around the world, scientists hope to monitor their health.

than you think.

The egg you grew from was formed when your mother was still in your grandmother's womb.

Egg

Sperm

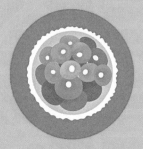

A baby is conceived when a father's sperm fertilizes a mother's egg. This forms a single cell called a **zygote**.

The zygote divides itself into lots of different cells and becomes an **embryo**.

The cells continue dividing and growing. After eight weeks, limbs and vital organs have developed. It is now known as a **fetus**.

The fetus grows inside the mother for 28 more weeks...

...and then the baby is born.

All of a woman's eggs are formed *while she is still a fetus*.

Men produce sperm throughout their adult lives.

So, you could say that part of you has existed since before your mother was born.

99 A sheet of pure gold...

can be so thin that it's transparent.

Pure gold is so soft that you can shape it with your bare hands. It is also extremely malleable – that is, it can be hammered into very, very thin sheets without cracking or tearing.

A piece of gold the size of a grain of rice...

...can be hammered into a sheet **11 square feet**. It would cover about 24 pages of this book.

Thin sheets of gold known as **gold leaf** have long been used to decorate valuable objects: books, paintings, statues and even buildings.

Gold can be made so thin that you can see through it. This has proved very useful to astronauts.

A film of gold just **0.000002 inches** thick is used as a transparent heat shield in the sun visors on astronauts' helmets.

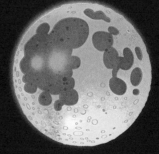

The gold visor reflects the Sun's hot infrared rays, but lets through enough green and blue light for the astronauts to see.

100 The internet...

is connected by millions of miles of cables.

The internet is a network that people use to share information. The first version, called the **Arpanet**, was invented in 1969.

4 out of **10** people in the world currently use the internet.

Internet speed is measured in megabits per second (Mbps). In 2019, South Korea became the first country to record an average speed of over **50 Mbps**.

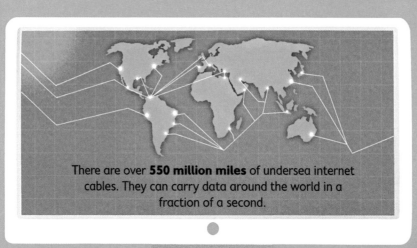

There are over **550 million miles** of undersea internet cables. They can carry data around the world in a fraction of a second.

There are over **22 billion devices** connected to the internet — nearly three times the total number of people in the world (7.8 billion).

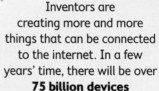

Inventors are creating more and more things that can be connected to the internet. In a few years' time, there will be over **75 billion devices** connected to the internet.

Glossary

This glossary explains some of the words used in this book. Words written in *italic* type have their own entries. For a glossary of scientific disciplines, turn to page 119.

acid A substance that *dissolves* in water and is often corrosive and sour-tasting; the chemical opposite of a *base*.

air resistance *Friction* caused by an object moving through air.

altitude The height of a thing or place above sea level.

Antarctic The icy region of Earth around the South Pole.

aquatic Anything in or to do with water.

Arctic The icy region of Earth around the North Pole.

atmosphere A mixture of gases that surrounds the Earth and other *planets*.

atom An incredibly tiny particle; the smallest building block of an *element*.

atomic matter Any substance made from *atoms*; virtually everything we can see.

atrophy When living *tissue* wastes away or breaks apart, it atrophies.

bacteria A type of *prokaryote*, usually only a few *cells* in size, that often lives inside other *organisms*.

base A substance that *dissolves* in water and is often corrosive and chalky tasting; the chemical opposite of an *acid*.

Big Bang, the A *theory* about how the *universe* began through the instantaneous appearance and rapid expansion of *matter* from an infinitesimally small point.

billion 1,000,000,000

cell The basic unit of living things.

climate change The way in which the average yearly temperature on Earth changes gradually over time.

clone An exact copy of a living thing.

colony A group of living things that live and work together, often unable to survive apart.

comet A ball of ice and dust in space that *orbits* a *star*.

computer A person or, more often, an *electronic machine* that processes *data*.

condense When a gas cools down and turns into a liquid, it condenses.

core The central part of a body such as a *planet*.

crater A hole in the surface of a planet or moon created by the impact of a lump of rock such as a meteor.

crust The solid surface layer of a *planet*, such as Earth.

data Information, especially that stored by *computers*.

dissolve When a solid substance merges into a liquid so that it can no longer be seen, it dissolves.

distillation A method of separating different substances by boiling them.

DNA A complex *molecule* found inside most *cells* that gives coded instructions to create a whole *organism*.

earthquake Waves of *energy* flowing through the ground, making the ground, and the things on it, shake.

electricity The flow of *energy* through a substance, carried by *electrons*, often used to transmit power to a *machine*.

electric charge The amount of power held by something that generates a flow of *electricity*, such as a battery.

electron An incredibly tiny *subatomic* particle normally found in a cloud at the edge of an *atom*. Clusters of electrons can produce certain effects such as a flow of *electricity*.

electronic Any machine powered by *electricity* flowing through circuits is electronic.

element A substance that is made up of just one kind of *atom*.

energy The power that makes things work. Heat, light, sound, motion and *electricity* are all forms of energy.

Equator An imaginary line around the middle of the Earth that divides the northern and southern *hemispheres*.

eruption An explosion from under the ground, either from a *volcano* or leading to the formation of a new volcano.

ESA European Space Agency, an organization dedicated to the exploration of space.

evaporation When a liquid turns into a gas without boiling.

evolution The gradual changes that all *organisms* undergo over generations, leading to the emergence of new *species*.

extinction When the last member of a *species* dies, that species becomes extinct.

fault Any place where separate sections of the Earth's *crust* can rub against each other, sometimes causing an *earthquake*.

force A push or pull that changes the motion or shape of an object.

fossil fuel A substance, such as crude oil, made from long-dead *organisms* and used to provide power.

foundations Parts of a building or other structure that are sunk into the ground to hold it in place.

friction A *force* caused when two things rub against each other.

fungi One of the five kingdoms of living things. The plural of *fungus*.

galaxy A collection of billions of *stars* that *orbit* together around a central hub.

gene A section of *DNA* that carries a code to define one or more specific characteristics of a living thing, such as its size.

global warming The very gradual rise in average yearly temperatures on Earth.

gravity The *force* of two objects pulling on each other; the force that keeps Earth in *orbit* around the Sun.

habitat The local environment in which an *organism* lives.

hemisphere Half of a sphere, often refers to the north and south halves of Earth.

immortal Describes an *organism* that will not die from natural causes.

infrared A kind of light that has slightly less *energy* than red light. It is invisible and not harmful to humans.

invertebrate A category of animals that have no backbone, such as insects.

laser A beam of intensely powerful light.

limestone A type of rock that *dissolves* gradually in rainwater, sometimes forming underground caves.

lunar Of, or to do with, the Moon.

machine A device that reduces the amount of *force* needed to move an object, or that changes the direction of the force applied.

magnet A metal object that attracts certain other metal objects.

magnetic field The area around a *magnet* in which objects are affected by that magnet's *force*.

magnetic poles The opposite ends of a *magnet*.

mammal A category of *vertebrates* that have hair, warm blood, and make milk for their babies.

mass The total amount of *atomic matter* inside a substance.

microbes Microscopic *organisms* such as *bacteria*.

microwave A type of *radiation* that makes water and some other *molecules* vibrate, causing them to heat up.

million 1,000,000

molecule Two or more *atoms* joined together make a molecule. Most substances are made of molecules rather than atoms.

moon A large rock that *orbits* a *planet*.

nanotube A microscopic man-made tube that can be just a few *atoms* wide.

NASA National Aeronautics and Space Administration, the U.S. government agency responsible for space exploration and research.

natural selection The process by which new *species* evolve from successful *organisms* – those organisms that are better suited to their *habitat*.

neuron A type of *cell* in the brain and spinal cord that passes information to other neurons.

neutral (*chemistry*) If a substance has a *pH* value of 7, it is neutral.

neutral (*electricity*) If an object has neither a positive nor a negative *electrical charge*, it is neutral.

neutron A *subatomic* particle with no *electrical charge*, usually found in the *nucleus* of an *atom*.

Nobel Prize A set of awards given out each year to people in various fields, including *physics*, *chemistry* and *medicine*.

nuclear bomb A bomb made of *radioactive* materials that explodes when the *atomic nuclei* in those materials break apart.

nuclear fission When the *nucleus* of an *atom* splits apart.

nuclear fusion When the *nuclei* of two or more *atoms* fuse together.

nuclear power A way to generate electricity by harnessing the heat given off as *radioactive* materials decay.

nuclei The plural of *nucleus*.

nucleus (atom) The central part of an *atom*.

nucleus (cell) A part found in most *cells* that contains *DNA*, and controls what the cell does.

nutrients The parts of food and drink that a living thing absorbs to stay alive.

observable universe, the A small part of the whole *universe*, that people can detect using instruments based on or around planet Earth.

orbit To travel through space around another, larger object.

organism Any living thing.

ozone A smelly type of oxygen that is abundant in the stratosphere.

pH Short for 'power of Hydrogen', a way to describe how *acidic* or *basic* a substance is.

photosynthesis The way in which plants and trees convert sunlight into *energy*.

piston A rod that moves back and forth, often to produce a pushing or pulling *force*.

planet A very large object in space that *orbits* around a *star*.

predator An animal that hunts and kills other animals to eat.

pressure The *force* applied by the surface of one object pushing on another.

primate Any member of the group of *mammals* that includes apes, monkeys and human beings.

probe An unmanned vehicle or machine used to explore a new place, such as space.

prokaryote The oldest known category of *organisms*, often made up of just a single type of *cell*.

protein A form of *nutrient* used to build different *tissues*.

protist A category of very small *organisms* made of multiple types of *cells*.

quintillion 1,000,000,000,000,000,000

radar A technique of scanning an area by sending out radio waves and analyzing the waves that bounce back.

radiation Particles or rays of *energy*, including heat and light, given off by a substance.

radioactivity When the atoms of a substance break apart and emit rays of harmful *radiation*.

solar power A method of converting *energy* from the Sun's light into *electricity*.

Solar System, the The collection of *planets*, *moons* and *asteroids* that *orbit* the Sun.

space station A man-made structure in space where people can live and work.

species A group of *organisms* that can breed with each other.

star An enormous object in space that continuously fuses its own *atoms* together, creating an incredibly powerful and long-lasting source of heat and light.

static electricity A build-up of *electric charge* in an object caused by some of its *atoms* gaining or losing *electrons*.

subatomic Smaller than an *atom*; relating to particles smaller than an atom.

tension The *force* exerted on an object by pulling on it from more than one side at the same time.

theory A scientific idea or explanation for how a process happened, or how it works, that can be tested by examining evidence and performing repeatable experiments.

tissue A substance that makes up a particular part of an *organism*, such as muscle tissue or bone tissue.

trillion 1,000,000,000,000

ultraviolet A type of light, invisible to human eyes, that can be harmful.

universe, the Everything that exists in time and space.

vertebrate A category of animals that have a backbone, such as birds, fish and *mammals*.

volcano A hole in the Earth's crust caused by an *eruption*, often inside a mountain formed from cooled lava.

Glossary of scientific disciplines

'Science' itself is not a single area of study. Most scientists study a general discipline, before specializing in a very specific area.

astronomy The study of outer space.

biology The study of living things.
  microbiology The study of tiny living things made of just one or a handful of cells.
  evolutionary biology The study of how *organisms* change over time.

botany The study of plants.

chemistry The study of substances – how they work, what they are made of and what they can do.
  biochemistry The chemistry of living things, especially the human body.

cosmology The study of how the *universe* began, and how it will end.

engineering Designing and building structures or *machines*.
  chemical engineering Creating new substances.
  mechanical engineering Creating new machines.

genetics The study of how *genes* affect living things.

geology The study of the Earth, especially its rocks.

medicine The study of how the human body works.

oceanography The study of the world's oceans and the things that live in them.

paleontology The study of *organisms* that lived in the distant past.

physics The study of how the world works, particularly the interaction of *forces* and *energy*.
  astrophysics The study of how *stars* work.
  nuclear physics The study of *subatomic* particles.

zoology The study of animals.

Timeline of recent scientific discoveries

Human beings have always investigated the world around them. This timeline shows just a handful of major discoveries in modern times. A huge breakthrough occurred in the early 17th century, when Italian astronomer Galileo Galilei studied outer space using a new invention – the telescope...

1600s
Galileo's observations confirmed that the Earth orbits the Sun.

1665
English philosopher **Robert Hooke** discovered the existence of cells using a microscope.

1676
Dutch lens maker **Antonie van Leeuwenhoek** discovered that microbes live in the human body.

1778
French chemist **Antoine Lavoisier** proved that oxygen is the source of fire.

1785
Scottish geologist **James Hutton** proposed that rock formations prove Earth is millions of years old.

1827
Scottish botanist **Robert Brown** watched the random movement of pollen grains in water, the first real evidence of atoms.

1856
The world's first oil refinery opened in Romania.

1926
Scottish inventor **John Logie Baird** demonstrated the first working television set.

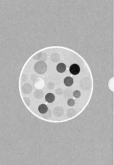

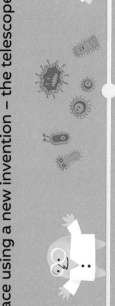

1930s
Austrian physicist **Lise Meitner** and German chemist **Otto Hahn** worked together to split an atom.

1944
A German V-2 rocket became the first man-made object to reach outer space.

1959
A Russian spacecraft circled and photographed the far side of the Moon.

1960
The submersible *Trieste* descended to the bottom of the deepest part of the ocean.

2014
ESA spacecraft *Rosetta* landed on a comet after a ten year journey.

2013
NASA space probe *Voyager 1* left the Solar System.

1996
Paleontologists in China uncovered the first firm evidence that some dinosaurs had feathers.

1991
British computer scientist **Tim Berners-Lee** made the World Wide Web publicly available.

Index

Internet links

For links to websites where you can discover more
surprising science facts, watch online experiments and
try test-yourself quizzes, go to the Usborne Quicklinks
website at **www.usborne.com/quicklinks** and enter
the keywords: **100 science things**.

Here are some of the things you can do at the
websites we recommend:

• Watch a dung beetle at work
• Discover inventions that have shaped your life
• See how a tsunami is formed
• Explore planets and other space objects
• Listen to sounds made by whales and fish

The recommended websites are regularly reviewed and updated
but, please note, Usborne Publishing is not responsible for the
content of any website other than its own. We recommend that
children are supervised while on the internet.

It took 20 people...
to put this book together.

Stage 1: Research and writing

4 authors compiled the 100 topics.

Alex Frith

Minna Lacey

Jerome Martin

Jonathan Melmoth

Stage 2: Design

4 designers laid out each page and made them pretty.

Matthew Bromley

Mary Cartwright

Lenka Hrehova

Stephen Moncrieff

Stage 3: Illustration

2 artists drew all the pictures.

Federico Mariani

Jorge Martin

Stage 4: Fact checking

6 experts checked all the topics for scientific accuracy.

Mark Champkins

Dr. Harry Cliff

Dr. Margaret & Dr. John Rostron

Dr. Kristina Routh

Dr. Roger Trend

Stage 5: Editing

4 editors ensured that each page made sense.

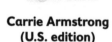

Ruth Brocklehurst

Jane Chisholm

Jenny Tyler

Carrie Armstrong
(U.S. edition)

Stage 6: Production

1 production controller organized the printing and binding of the book in your hands.

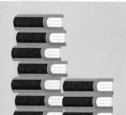

Lauren Easey